COMMON CORE WRITING PROMPTS AND STRATEGIES

A SUPPLEMENT TO
CIVIL RIGHTS
HISTORICAL INVESTIGATIONS

Facing History & Ourselves uses lessons of history to challenge teachers and their students to stand up to racism, antisemitism, and other forms of bigotry and hate. For more information about Facing History & Ourselves, please visit our website at www.facinghistory.org.

Copyright © 2015 by Facing History & Ourselves, Inc. All rights reserved.

Facing History & Ourselves® is a trademark registered in the US Patent & Trademark Office.

Last updated May 2025.

ISBN: 978-1-940457-12-3

CONTENTS

How to Use This Resource. 5
Teaching Writing Is Teaching Thinking. 6
Argumentative Writing: Research and Directions in Learning and Teaching 9

PROMPTS AND STRATEGIES 17

STRATEGIES TO USE BEFORE STARTING *CIVIL RIGHTS HISTORICAL INVESTIGATIONS* 18

A. Understanding the Prompt. 18
   Strategy 1. Anticipation Guides* and Four Corners Discussion 19
   Strategy 2. Dissecting the Prompt 22
   Strategy 3. Defining Key Terms* 23
   Strategy 4. Journal Suggestions* 31

STRATEGIES TO USE DURING THE STUDY OF *CIVIL RIGHTS HISTORICAL INVESTIGATIONS* . . . 33

B. Gathering and Analyzing Evidence 33
   Strategy 5. Evidence Logs and Index Cards* 34
   Strategy 6. Annotating and Paraphrasing Sources 42
   Strategy 7. Collecting and Sharing Evidence 44
      a. Gallery Walk 44
      b. Give One, Get One 45
      c. Two-Minute Interview 45
   Strategy 8. Evaluating Evidence 48
   Strategy 9. Relevant or Not? 50
   Strategy 10. Learning to Infer 52
   Strategy 11. Assessing Source Credibility 54
   Strategy 12. Successful Online Research 57

STRATEGIES TO USE AFTER COMPLETING *CIVIL RIGHTS HISTORICAL INVESTIGATIONS*, WHILE WRITING FORMAL ESSAY 58

C. Crafting a Thesis and Organizing Ideas 58
   Strategy 13. Taking a Stand on Controversial Issues: Speaking and Listening
   Strategies 59
      a. Barometer 59
      b. SPAR (Spontaneous Argumentation) 60
      c. Final Word 60
   Strategy 14. Building Arguments through Mini-Debates 62
   Strategy 15. Linking Claims and Evidence with Analysis 65

  Strategy 16. Thesis Sorting. 67
  Strategy 17. Tug for Truth 69
  Strategy 18. Refuting Counterarguments. 70
D. Proving Your Point through Logical Reasoning in Body Paragraphs 72
  Strategy 19. Claims, Data, and Analysis 73
  Strategy 20. Using Exemplars (or Mentor Texts) 76
  Strategy 21. Looking at Student Work: Body Paragraphs 77
  Strategy 22. Using Graphic Organizers to Organize Writing 80
  Strategy 23. Sentence-Strip Paragraphs 85
E. Framing and Connecting Ideas in Introductions and Conclusions 87
  Strategy 24. Introductions: Inverted Pyramid. 88
  Strategy 25. Conclusions: Text-to-Text, Text-to-Self, Text-to-World. 90
  Strategy 26. Fishbowl. 91
  Strategy 27. Writing Conclusions after Looking at Student Samples . . . 93
F. Revising and Editing to Impact Your Audience 96
  Strategy 28. 3-2-1 97
  Strategy 29. Adding Transitions 98
  Strategy 30. Backwards Outline 99
  Strategy 31. Conferring. 102
  Strategy 32. Read-Alouds 104
G. Publishing/Sharing/Reflecting 105
  Strategy 33. Reflecting on the Process 106
  Strategy 34. Online Publishing. 107

APPENDIX. 109

Sample Road Map for *Civil Rights Historical Investigations* and the Common Core. 109
English Language Arts Standards, Writing in History/Social Studies 113
English Language Arts Standards, Reading in History/Social Studies. 116
English Language Arts Standards, Speaking and Listening. 118
Sample High School Rubric for Argumentative Writing Prompts. 120

*Indicates strategies that are specific to a particular writing prompt.

HOW TO USE THIS RESOURCE

This resource is to support you, the teacher in a Facing History & Ourselves classroom, as you help your students become stronger analytical thinkers and writers. It includes materials to supplement the *Civil Rights Historical Investigations* unit with a formal argumentative essay.

The materials include the following:

- an overview of current research about argumentative writing that was used to inform this work
- specific writing prompts
- thinking/writing strategies appropriate for both history and language arts classrooms
- explicit alignment with the expectations of the Common Core Standards for Literacy in History/Social Studies

We do not expect that you will use every strategy in every section. That would be time-consuming and redundant. Each section includes many strategies that target similar thinking and writing skills. We encourage you to choose one or several in each section that best fit your students' needs.

The strategies are organized into sections labeled by the types of thinking. The sections are organized into three main groups:

- strategies to use *before* you begin your study of *Civil Rights Historical Investigations*,
- strategies to use *during* your study, and
- strategies to use *after* completing *Civil Rights Historical Investigations*, while writing a formal essay.

TEACHING WRITING IS TEACHING THINKING

Helping students express themselves has always been central to Facing History's mission and curriculum. Writing—exploratory, formal, playful, provocative—helps students to engage self and others and to deepen their understanding about important historical content and themes. Teaching writing will empower you to engage students both with the big ideas of history and with the power of their own minds.

Fundamentally, teaching writing is teaching thinking. That is something Facing History teachers already value. We hope you will find that this resource enhances and extends your existing expertise.

Thinking and Writing

Thinking and writing have rich connections; one does not precede the other. As historian Lynn Hunt says, "Writing means many different things to me but one thing it is not: writing is not the transcription of thoughts already consciously present in my mind. Writing is a magical and mysterious process that makes it possible to think differently."[1] This is equally true whether one "writes" the old-fashioned way (putting pen to paper) or composes and reworks ideas with the use of electronic technologies.

About the Writing Prompts

Fundamentally, if students are to be strong writers, they need to be strong analytical thinkers. And they need content worth thinking about.[2] We had this in mind when designing the specific writing prompts. Note that the prompts

- serve as essential questions for students to revisit throughout a unit;
- correspond to aspects of the Facing History journey;
- engage students ethically, intellectually, and emotionally;
- address core concepts—such as significance, causation, agency, evidence, and continuity and change—that allow students to build historical understanding;
- demand the sort of text-dependent analysis recommended in the Common Core Standards.

Patterns of Thinking Students Use When Crafting Written Arguments

This resource is divided into seven sections, based on patterns of thinking that historians (and other scholars) use when analyzing content and crafting written arguments. The goal is to support students in their thinking and in the clear expression of that thinking for a specific purpose and audience. This approach differs considerably from the generic and outdated concept of "the" writing process.

---

1 Lynn Hunt, "How Writing Leads to Thinking (And Not the Other Way Around)," The Art of History, *Perspectives Online*, February 2010, http://www.historians.org/perspectives/issues/2010/1002/1002art1.cfm.

2 George Hillocks, *Research on Written Composition: New Directions for Teaching* (Urbana, IL: ERIC Clearinghouse on Reading and Communication Skills and the National Conference on Research in English, 1986).

A. Understanding the Prompt

In order to write a strong essay, students need to know what they are being asked to think about and need to have something to say.[3] One challenge for many student writers is that they lack sufficient understanding of the content. As Joan Didion once stated, "I write entirely to find out what I'm thinking, what I'm looking at, what I see, and what it means."[4] The strategies in Section A are designed to help students engage with the big moral issues they will write about formally later. Note that many of the strategies in Section A *are* writing—early, exploratory, messy writing to help students formulate and develop lines of thought.

B. Gathering and Analyzing Evidence

The strategies in Section B help students think about *what* they are reading and learning. Historical reasoning requires students to focus on evidence, perspective, and interpretation.[5] By careful and close reading of a wide variety of primary and secondary sources, students begin to develop their own arguments. They learn to examine evidence carefully to determine whether it is accurate, credible, and persuasive.[6] Note that these strategies help students engage with the evidence, and they *precede* the work of actually synthesizing the evidence and crafting a thesis statement.

C. Crafting a Thesis and Organizing Ideas

Much of historical thinking and writing involves forming strong arguments or interpretations based on the core concepts in history: Why does this matter? How did this happen? What motivated people in the past to think and act in the ways they did? How do we know what we know? How was this past situation similar to present-day situations? Fundamentally, the strategies in Section C help students learn to sort out "What is *my* perspective on this issue?" Note that we placed crafting a thesis *after* students have many opportunities to examine the evidence. A recent study found that college professors express concern that many students leap to writing a thesis before they have explored their ideas in sufficient detail.[7] Here, crafting a thesis and organizing ideas are paired, as a way to help students begin to integrate, synthesize, and categorize their ideas.

D. Proving Your Point through Logical Reasoning in Body Paragraphs

Argumentative essays typically have one central argument (the thesis or central claim) and multiple smaller arguments in which the author presents a claim or reason, cites evidence, and offers analysis. This analysis, technically called a warrant,

---

[3] Hillocks, *Research on Written Composition*.

[4] Joan Didion, "Why I Write," *New York Times Magazine,* December 5, 1976, 270.

[5] Chauncey Monte-Sano, "Beyond Reading Comprehension and Summary: Learning to Read and Write in History by Focusing on Evidence, Perspective, and Interpretation," *Curriculum Inquiry* 41, no. 2 (2011): 212-249.

[6] Chauncey Monte-Sano, "Disciplinary Literacy in History: An Exploration of the Historical Nature of Adolescents' Writing," *Journal of the Learning Sciences* 19, no. 4 (2010): 539-568.

[7] Stevi Quate, ed., "Lessons Learned: A Report of the DASSC Writing Inquiry Project," June 1, 2011, http://writinginquiry.wikispaces.com/file/view/Lessonslearned.pdf.

is the glue holding claims and evidence together.[8] In this section, we include strategies to help students practice orally linking claims, evidence, and analysis. We also include ways to help students learn more flexible ways to present those ideas so their writing feels fresh, not formulaic.

E. Framing and Connecting Ideas in Introductions and Conclusions

Facing History aims for students to make connections between history and the choices they make in their own lives. We believe that students are most engaged when they are stimulated intellectually, emotionally, and ethically. When writing a formal/academic argumentative essay, students demonstrate that they can make these big conceptual connections mostly in the opening and closing paragraphs. In this section, we include strategies that support students in first *making* those connections to the here and now and then expressing those connections in ways that are clear and compelling to their audience.

F. Revising and Editing to Impact Your Audience

Students can substantially improve their logic and expression when they receive clear, specific, constructive feedback.[9] They also become better readers of their own writing when they analyze and critique others' writing—both "mentor texts" from the real world[10] and their peers' writing. During the revising stage, students clarify, reorganize, and strengthen the content of their paper. This section provides two sorts of strategies to revise or "rework" earlier writing: peer feedback and self-assessment. While Facing History sees the importance of copyediting one's writing to address grammar, spelling, or punctuation errors, in this resource we emphasize the broader challenges of helping students effectively develop and express their reasoning.

G. Publishing/Sharing/Reflecting

Thinkers write for many purposes; the purpose of formal writing is to express an idea to an audience. It is important to end the CWA process with an opportunity for students to share what they wrote with their peers or an outside audience. In this section, we include strategies and suggestions for how students can make their thinking public. We also include ways that students can think about what they learned about the topic and about themselves as writers.

---

8 Andrea A. Lunsford and John J. Ruszkiewicz, *Everything's an Argument,* 2nd ed. (New York: Bedford/St. Martin's, 2001), 95.

9 Richard Beach and Tom Friedrich, "Response to Writing," in *Handbook of Writing Research,* ed. C. A. McArthur, S. Graham, and J. Fitzgerald (New York: The Guilford Press, 2006), 222–234.

10 Katie Wood Ray, *Study Driven: A Framework for Planning Units of Study in the Writing Workshop* (Portsmouth, NH: Heinemann, 2006).

ARGUMENTATIVE WRITING: RESEARCH AND DIRECTIONS IN LEARNING AND TEACHING

The following document is meant to help you understand current trends and directions in the research around teaching argumentative writing in history. Facing History & Ourselves is concerned with many aspects of a learner's identity—from moral philosopher to analytical thinker to ethical decision maker to historical reasoner—and recognizes the need for our students to become profound thinkers and writers. The following information is intended to help you consider how to support your students in this journey.

I. What We Want for Our Students as Thinkers and Writers

Growth Mindset and Writers' Dispositions

Recent research by Dweck[11] indicates that people can hold two different beliefs, or "mindsets," about intelligence: the "fixed" mindset (in which people believe they either are smart or stupid, good or bad at specific skills) and the "growth" mindset (in which people believe they can get better at things and are always learning). Facing History & Ourselves fully embraces the growth mindset; we hope to encourage students and teachers to see students through that lens.

Experts in the field of writing instruction indicate that in order for students to succeed as writers in college and careers, they need certain dispositions, perhaps even more than specific skills. These dispositions include curiosity; engagement; appreciation of craft; ability to reflect, analyze, synthesize, and revise; willingness to give and receive feedback; persistence in moving beyond the self; and valuing reading and writing as powerful tools for inquiry.[12]

When teaching writing, help students know that all writers are always learning and growing. Writing is *not* something you either "can" or "can't" do, something you are either "good at" or "bad at." Support and celebrate students' curiosity, persistence, and willingness to reflect on their own thinking and writing. Given Facing History's focus on intellectual, social, and moral development, we encourage teachers to "teach the writer, not the writing."[13] Help them learn about themselves as writers in ways that allow them to transfer that learning to future writing tasks and other life challenges.

Argument

Students demonstrate their strong analytical thinking by crafting oral and written arguments. These skills are emphasized in the Common Core Standards for Literacy in History/Social Studies. Specifically, Writing Anchor Standard 1 demands that students write arguments on discipline-specific content within a history classroom.

---

[11] Carol S. Dweck, *Mindset: The New Psychology of Success* (New York: Ballantine Books, 2008).

[12] Quate, "Lessons Learned" and "Framework for Success in Postsecondary Writing," CWPA, NCTE, and NWP, January 2011, http://wpacouncil.org/files/framework-for-success-postsecondary-writing.pdf.

[13] Lucy Calkins, *The Art of Teaching Writing* (Portsmouth, NH: Heinemann, 1994).

This is not to be confused with merely writing a persuasive essay; the Common Core State Standards Initiative (CCSSI) focuses on text-based historical writing that argues for a point of view.

The most commonly referenced model for written argument was developed by Stephen Toulmin.[14] Toulmin described six key elements/concepts with which an argument can be analyzed and constructed.[15]

> ***Claim:*** the statement you are asking others to accept
>
> ***Grounds:*** the basis of persuasion; the data, evidence, and reasons
>
> ***Warrant:*** the link or "glue" that holds the evidence and claim together[16], explaining how and why the evidence helps prove the claim
>
> ***Backing:*** the additional support for the warrant
>
> ***Qualifier:*** indicates strength of the leap from claim to warrant; may limit universality of the claims
>
> ***Rebuttal:*** acknowledgment of counterarguments; typically includes own claims, grounds, warrants

The CCSSI notes,

> Crafting an argument frequently relies on using information; similarly, an analysis of a subject will likewise include argumentative elements. While these forms are not strictly independent, what is critical to both forms of writing is the use and integration of evidence. In historical, technical, and scientific writing, accuracy matters, and students should demonstrate their knowledge through precision and detail.[17]

Persuasion is a *subset* of argument, in which authors intentionally use rhetorical devices to compel their readers.[18] There are different types of argument, including those based on facts and reason, character, and values. Facing History emphasizes both reasoning and empathy when crafting written arguments and wants students to find their voice and claim their power by being able to argue for a point of view. At the heart of argument is the relationship between claims, grounds (evidence), and warrants (analysis). Students may better understand the kind of thinking you want them to do if you show them this visual and teach them the "language" of argument. Many students struggle when learning to craft effective analysis/warrants. Students need to make explicit to their audience how the evidence supports the claim, rather than expecting readers to infer.

Critical Thinking

To be engaged citizens, students need to be able to analyze, question, and critique texts.[19] At Facing History, we encourage teachers to use learning-centered teaching

---

14 Stephen Toulmin, *The Uses of Argument* (Cambridge, UK: Cambridge University Press, 1958).

15 "Toulmin's Argument Model," accessed October 22, 2011, http://changingminds.org/disciplines/argument/making_argument/toulmin.htm.

16 Lunsford and Ruszkiewicz, *Everything's an Argument*, 95.

17 "Draft Publisher's Criteria for the Common Core State Standards in ELA & Literacy, Grades 4–12," accessed October 22, 2011, http://www.ode.state.or.us/wma/teachlearn/commoncore/ela-publishers-criteria.pdf.

18 Lunsford and Ruszkiewicz, *Everything's an Argument*.

19 M. McLaughlin and G. DeVoogd, "Critical Literacy as Comprehension: Expanding Reader Response," *Journal of*

strategies that nurture students' literacy and critical thinking skills within a respectful classroom culture.

As defined by experts in the field of literacy,

> *Critical thinking* is the ability to analyze a situation or text and make thoughtful decisions based on that analysis. Writers use critical writing and reading to develop and represent the processes and products of their critical thinking. For example, writers may be asked to write about familiar or unfamiliar texts, examining assumptions about the texts held by different audiences. Through critical writing and reading, writers think through ideas, problems, and issues; identify and challenge assumptions; and explore multiple ways of understanding.[20]

Teachers can help writers develop critical thinking by providing opportunities and guidance to

- read texts from multiple points of view;
- write about texts for multiple purposes, including (but not limited to) interpretation, synthesis, response, summary, critique, and analysis;
- craft written responses to texts that put the writer's ideas in conversation with those in a text;
- evaluate sources for credibility, bias, quality of evidence, and quality of reasoning;
- conduct primary and secondary research using a variety of print and nonprint sources;
- write texts for various audiences and purposes that are informed by research (e.g., to support ideas or positions, to illustrate alternative perspectives); and
- generate questions to guide research.[21]

Facing History has always emphasized critical thinking as a cornerstone of civic engagement. One can only engage with society if one asks the hard questions and views issues from many angles.

Historical Reasoning ("Disciplinary Literacy")

Students in Facing History classrooms have myriad opportunities to develop their general analytical thinking skills. They also have an opportunity to develop more specific "historical reasoning."[22]

Literacy scholars have begun to focus on this idea of "disciplinary literacy": the advanced, specialized literacies required for one to read, write, and think about specific content in ways most valued by a given academic discipline[23] and that

---

Adolescent and Adult Literacy 48, no. 1 (2004): 52–62.

20 "Framework for Success," CWPA, NCTE, and NWP.

21 Ibid.

22 Monte-Sano, "Beyond Reading Comprehension."

23 Elizabeth Birr Moje et al., "Integrating Literacy Instruction into Secondary School Science Inquiry: The Challenges of Disciplinary Literacy Teaching and Professional Development," accessed October 22, 2011, http://

advance disciplinary understanding.[24] Monte-Sano has researched the disciplinary literacy specific to "historical writing" (when students write arguments about historical events) and states the following:

- "Historical reasoning involves reading evidence from the perspective of those who created it and placing it into context. Such contextualization is central to history, in that historians may only interrogate artifacts from the past";[25]

- "In constructing historical arguments, writing is often inextricable from a disciplinary way of thinking and working with evidence. According to history experts, the use and framing of evidence in historical writing indicate key aspects of disciplinary reasoning, including recognizing biases in sources, comparing evidence, situating evidence in its context, and taking into account different perspectives and multiple causes";[26]

- Strong use of evidence in historical writing includes the following "benchmarks"[27]:
    » **Factual and interpretive accuracy:** offering evidence that is correct and interpretations that are plausible
    » **Persuasiveness of evidence:** including evidence that is relevant and strong in terms of helping to prove the claim
    » **Sourcing of evidence:** noting what the source is and its credibility and/or bias
    » **Corroboration of evidence:** recognizing how different documents work together to support a claim
    » **Contextualization of evidence:** placing the evidence into its appropriate historical context

Facing History materials invite and require strong historical reasoning, since students are required to examine evidence carefully, consider the assumptions and bias of specific authors or sources, and consistently come to strong interpretations about historical events.

II. What This Means for Our Teaching

Teach Writing Processes

Anyone who has written—whether composing with traditional pen and paper or with the use of electronic technologies—knows that writing is messy, complex, and anything but linear. Students engage in myriad cognitive activities as they write.

---

www-personal.umich.edu/~moje/pdf/MojeEtAlScienceLiteracyTeachingStrategies2010.pdf, and Timothy Shanahan and Cynthia Shanahan, "Teaching Disciplinary Literacy to Adolescents: Rethinking Content-Area Literacy," *Harvard Educational Review* 78, no. 1 (2008), 40–59.

24 Monte-Sano, "Beyond Reading Comprehension," 218.
25 Monte-Sano, "Disciplinary Literacy in History," 541.
26 Monte-Sano, "Disciplinary Literacy in History."
27 Benchmarks of strong use of evidence developed by Monte-Sano, based on prior thinking of Wineburg (199) as found in Monte-Sano, "Beyond Reading Comprehension," 213. Monte-Sano, "Disciplinary Literacy in History."

Scholars no longer think of "the" singular linear writing process. Rather, the process is multifaceted and recursive.[28] As stated recently in the framework prepared by three leading writing organizations:

> *Writing processes* are the multiple strategies writers use to approach and undertake writing and research. Writing processes are not linear. Successful writers use different processes that vary over time and depend on the particular task. For example, a writer may research a topic before drafting, then after receiving feedback conduct additional research as part of revising. Writers learn to move back and forth through different stages of writing, adapting those stages to the situation. This ability to employ flexible writing processes is important as students encounter different types of writing tasks.[29]

Students need to learn to toggle back and forth between the messy thinking and putting that thinking into a coherent and clear written form. They also need to practice key rhetorical concepts to help them understand *why* they are writing. They need help thinking about concepts such as audience, purpose, context, and genre.[30] We see this writing as a crucial part of the journey of a Facing History student; it is a process where students test their assumptions and routinely reevaluate their ideas, thinking critically about the information they are studying and communicating these thoughts to the world around them.

Use Inquiry; Embed Authentic Experiences and Explicit Instruction

Overall, Facing History takes an inquiry approach: the curriculum is designed to engage students in the moral and philosophical questions regarding historical events and individual choices within a developmental context. Researchers have found that a similar "inquiry-based" mode of writing instruction has the greatest effects on student achievement.[31] Basically, this means that the teacher provides clear and specific objectives about the writing, chooses rich materials to engage students in the *thinking* that sits underneath the writing, and creates activities like small-group problem-centered discussions that invite high levels of peer interaction. This inquiry mode is in contrast to both the "presentation" mode (lecturing students on how to write) and the "natural process" mode (learning writing by doing, with little explicit instruction).

In the field of writing research, scholars debate how people learn language forms—such as argumentative writing—that are not their primary discourse.[32] Some argue that secondary discourses can't be taught and are best learned "through experience by participating in situated use of particular language forms." Others argue that language is best learned "through tutelage and explicit instruction in its structures and forms."[33]

---

28 Gert Rijlaarsdam and Huub van den Bergh, "Writing Process Theory: A Functional Dynamic Approach" in *Handbook of Writing Research*, ed. Charles A. MacArthur, Steve Graham, and Jill Fitzgerald. (New York: The Guilford Press, 2006), 51.

29 "Framework for Success," CWPA, NCTE, and NWP.

30 Ibid.

31 Hillocks, *Research on Written Composition*.

32 Gee, J. P. "The social Mind: Language, Ideology, and Social Practice," Series in Language and Ideology (New York: Bergin & Garvey, 1992).

33 Victoria Purcell-Gates, Nell K. Duke, and Joseph A. Martineau, "Learning to Read and Write Genre-Specific Text:

The middle ground asserts that "language is best learned through a combination . . . of [authentic] experience and explicit instruction" about the specific techniques or "moves" writers make.[34] As Lisa Delpit states, "Merely adopting direct instruction is not the answer. Actual writing for real audiences and real purposes is a vital element in helping students to understand that they have an important voice in their own learning process."[35]

To honor inquiry and authenticity, Facing History has created essential questions directly linked to the writing prompts that help frame students' inquiry for the unit. We have built in many opportunities for students to engage in the thinking related to writing in small-group problem-solving/inquiry contexts. And we include strategies for explicit teaching of argument and historical reasoning, and how to transfer that thinking into a final written essay.

Model and Provide Mentor Texts

Just as students benefit from seeing more skilled athletes or musicians as they are learning a sport or instrument, students benefit from seeing real writers at work as they learn to write argumentative essays. In the field of writing instruction, this includes both the use of "mentor texts"[36] and use of teacher or peer models of *how* you are crafting a piece of writing.

Fundamentally, the use of mentor texts invites students to "notice and name" the particular techniques a writer has used to have an effect on an audience. Students come to understand more about the criteria for good writing from actually *analyzing* good writing than from simply reading a rubric. Reading others' writing through this lens helps students think about the writer's purpose, and the *ideas* presented in the piece, and <u>then</u> to think about the specific techniques the writer used to have an impact on the reader. In this resource, we include examples of argumentative essays that your students can read, analyze, critique, revise, and emulate.

Students also benefit from seeing writers in process. Studies indicate that when teachers show students how they cope with problems as writers, students make gains. By modeling for students how you actually move through the challenges of writing an argumentative essay, you offer students metacognitive language of self-assessment and revision.[37]

Feedback and Self-Assessment

Facing History has designed assignments that invite alternative perspectives, and thus invite students to revise their thinking.[38] In order to do so, students need clear, specific, constructive feedback. Students need to communicate clearly and

---

Roles of Authentic Experience and Explicit Teaching," *Reading Research Quarterly* 42, no. 1 (Jan/Feb/March 2007), 8–45, and Steven Graham, "Strategy Instruction and the Teaching of Writing: A Meta-Analysis," in *Handbook of Writing Research*, ed. C. A. McArthur, S. Graham, and J. Fitzgerald (New York: The Guilford Press, 2006). 222–234.

34 Purcell-Gates, Duke, and Martineau, "Genre-Specific Text," 8.

35 Lisa D. Delpit, "The Silenced Dialogue: Power and Pedagogy in Educating Other People's Children," in Landmark Essays in Basic Writing, ed. Kay Halasek and Nels P. Highberg (Mahwah, NJ: Lawrence Earlbaum Associates, 2001).

36 Katie Wood Ray, *Study Driven*.

37 Beach and Friedrich, "Response to Writing," 227.

38 Ibid.

respectfully with peers about how they might improve their writing. And ultimately, students need to become metacognitive, conscious of their own writing choices and challenges and able to independently self-assess and improve their own writing.

Scholar Brian Cambourne found that children most easily acquire early facility with oral and written language when certain "conditions" exist.[39] One of those conditions is "response": listening to students' thinking, welcoming their comments and questions, and extending their use of written and oral language.[40] The same is true for adolescents. Students need to know that their thinking is valued. They also benefit from specific response.

There is some disagreement in the field about whether a "direct" stance (telling students what to fix) or an "indirect" stance (telling students your actual thinking about their thinking) helps writers improve more. Some specific findings regarding feedback on student writing include:[41]

- Written comments are often too vague or global.
- Students value audio-taped comments, which seem more authentic, as if the reader is in dialogue with the writer.
- All students, particularly English-language learners, benefit from one-on-one conferences about their writing. Conferring helps students verbalize their thoughts, helps teachers introduce specialized vocabulary, and allows teachers to ask probing questions to help students clarify their thinking.
- Peer feedback is helpful if peers are taught to provide specific, descriptive feedback and have good process skills to collaborate.
- Students like teachers to correct their errors (since it is more efficient) but need to learn to correct their own.

In Facing History classrooms, students are encouraged to revise their thinking as well as their writing. Teachers can support students as thinkers and writers by responding authentically to their ideas and by giving specific recommendations on how to convey those ideas more effectively. They can also help peers learn to do this with and for one another.

Conclusion

As Ted Sizer stated in the introduction to the book *The Right to Literacy in Secondary Schools* by Suzanne Plaut, "Literacy... is the fuel for freedom." Plaut herself goes to say that literacy is "a social imperative... [which] enables students to have a voice, take a stand, and make a difference. In other words, it gives them power."[42]

We believe that by teaching argumentation and critical thinking in your classroom through the lens of writing, thinking, and discussion, you will be giving students tools to access freedom, power, and civic agency.

---

39 Brian Cambourne, *The Whole Story: Natural Learning and the Acquisition of Literacy in the Classroom* (Jefferson, MO: Scholastic, 1988).

40 Elizabeth Lilly and Connie Green, *Developing Partnerships with Families through Children's Literature,* 2004 ed. (Boston: Prentice Hall, 2004), 5.

41 Beach and Friedrich, "Response to Writing."

42 Suzanne N. Plaut, *The Right to Literacy in Secondary Schools: Creating a Culture of Thinking* (New York: Teachers College Press, 2009).

In the curriculum materials that follow, we have tried to find intersections between Facing History & Ourselves pedagogy, analytical thinking, and argumentative writing to help you on your journey as a Facing History teacher.

PROMPTS AND STRATEGIES

ARGUMENTATIVE WRITING PROMPTS

Below you will find three **argumentative writing prompts** to use with *Civil Rights Historical Investigations*. For each prompt, we have also included an **essential question**. This question is distinct from the prompt; it is a **theme** to explore throughout your Facing History unit. The essential question helps guide you and your students in thinking about big ideas connected to the prompt. We recommend using the essential question throughout the unit but focusing on the specific prompt when teaching writing strategies.

Prompt #1

Essential Question: *How is the struggle against the forces of injustice to be waged?*

> In the essay "Nonviolence and Racial Justice" (1957), Martin Luther King, Jr., asks, "How is the struggle against the forces of injustice to be waged?"
>
> Answer his question by arguing which strategies best helped civil rights activists achieve the goal of overcoming injustice. Draw on specific evidence from the civil rights movement to support your answer.

Prompt #2

Essential Question: *How powerful are we?*

> *An individual is powerless to change society.*
>
> *An individual has the power to change society.*
>
> Which statement does the history of the civil rights movement most support? Draw on specific evidence from the civil rights movement to support your answer.

Prompt #3

Essential Question: *What changes the world?*

> Anthropologist Margaret Mead said, "Never doubt that a small group of thoughtful, committed citizens can change the world. Indeed, it is the only thing that ever has."
>
> Support, refute, or modify this statement based on specific evidence from the history of the civil rights movement.

STRATEGIES TO USE BEFORE STARTING *CIVIL RIGHTS HISTORICAL INVESTIGATIONS*

A. UNDERSTANDING THE PROMPT

*Use these strategies **before** starting the unit.*

In order to write a strong essay, students need to know what they are being asked to think about and need to have something to say.[1] One challenge for many student writers is that they lack sufficient understanding of the content. As Joan Didion once stated, "I write entirely to find out what I'm thinking, what I'm looking at, what I see, and what it means."[2] The strategies in Section A are designed to help students understand the historical content and big ideas that they will write about formally later.

The prompts serve as essential questions for students to revisit throughout the Facing History unit. Each prompt corresponds to an aspect of the Facing History journey; engages students ethically, intellectually and emotionally; addresses core concepts in history—such as significance, causation, agency, evidence, and continuity and change—and demands the sort of text-dependent analysis recommended in the Common Core Standards. Teachers can choose one prompt as the big idea for the unit or let students choose which prompt to write about. Teachers are also encouraged to break down the prompts even further if working with English-language learners or other students who may need more scaffolding.

Note that many of the strategies to help students understand the prompt *are* writing—early, exploratory, messy writing to help students formulate and develop lines of thought. Other strategies are oral, since most students also benefit from having multiple opportunities to "talk through" their ideas with peers.[3]

---

1 George Hillocks, *Research on Written Composition: New Directions for Teaching* (Urbana, IL: ERIC Clearinghouse on Reading and Communication Skills and the National Conference on Research in English, 1986).

2 Joan Didion, "Why I Write," *New York Times Magazine,* December 5, 1976, 270.

3 Martin Nystrand, Adam Gamoran, and William Carbonaro, "Towards an Ecology or Learning: The Case of Classroom Discourse and Its Effects on Writing in High School English and Social Studies" (Center on English Learning & Achievement, Report Number 11001, 1998), accessed October 22, 2011, http://www.albany.edu/cela/reports/nystrand/nystrandtowards11001.pdf.

STRATEGY 1. Anticipation Guides and Four Corners Discussion

WRITING FOCUS: Develop opinions about controversial topics.

COMMON CORE ALIGNMENT: Write arguments focused on discipline-specific content. (WHST.9-10.1)

RATIONALE

Having students share responses to controversial statements can engage students with the writing prompt and help them think about the topic in a nuanced way. Students can return to these same statements after their study of the civil rights movement to see how learning this material has reinforced or shifted their earlier beliefs.

PROCEDURE

1. Pass out the Anticipation Guide that relates to the specific prompt (**Reproducible 1.1** or **1.2**).

2. Ask students to read each statement and decide if they strongly agree, agree, disagree, or strongly disagree with each statement. They should circle their response and then write a brief explanation for their choice.

3. After students have filled out their guides, organize the room into four corners. Each corner should have one of the following four signs: "strongly agree," "agree," "disagree," and "strongly disagree."

4. Next, use the "Four Corners" strategy to share ideas. Read each statement aloud and ask students to stand in the corner that best represents their current thinking. After students move, ask them to talk to others in their corner to explain their thinking to each other.

5. Next, ask students in each corner to share their ideas with the rest of the class. As one corner disagrees with another, encourage students to respond directly to each other's statements and have a mini-debate about the prompt. If, due to the debate, students' ideas changes, tell them they are free to switch corners.

6. At the end of the activity, introduce students to the prompt and/or essential question. Ask students to journal their current answer to the prompt and essential question. They can incorporate the discussions from the anticipation guide activity or simply write what they think.

7. Tell students that they will return to these ideas as they learn about the history of the civil rights movement. They can keep all their notes about these ideas in their interactive notebooks.

REPRODUCIBLE 1.1 Anticipation Guide for Prompt #1

Read the statement in the left column. Decide if you strongly agree (SA), agree (A), disagree (D), or strongly disagree (SD) with the statement. Circle your response and provide a one- to two-sentence explanation of your opinion.

Statements	Your opinion			
1. The only people who can challenge injustice are people in power, like the President of the United States.	SA Explain:	A	D	SD
2. The struggle against the forces of injustice should be waged with violence.	SA Explain:	A	D	SD
3. The Supreme Court is most responsible for correcting injustice in our society.	SA Explain:	A	D	SD
4. To end injustice, we need to use strategies such as organizing, protesting, and marching.	SA Explain:	A	D	SD
5. If there is injustice in my community, I usually ignore it and wait for someone in power to deal with it.	SA Explain:	A	D	SD
6. In a democracy, citizens are responsible for creating the just society that they want to live in.	SA Explain:	A	D	SD
7. "Injustice anywhere is a threat to justice everywhere." (–MLK, Jr.)	SA Explain:	A	D	SD
8. If my friend faces injustice, I feel compelled to do something about it.	SA Explain:	A	D	SD

REPRODUCIBLE 1.2 Anticipation Guide for Prompt #2

Read the statement in the left column. Decide if you strongly agree (SA), agree (A), disagree (D), or strongly disagree (SD) with the statement. Circle your response.

Statement	Your opinion			
1. Youth only have the power to change society when they work with adults; on their own, young people are powerless to create change.	SA Explain:	A	D	SD
2. Any young person has the power to change society for the better and for the worse.	SA Explain:	A	D	SD
3. Leaders are the only individuals who have the power to change society; young people are powerless to change society.	SA Explain:	A	D	SD
4. The president is not as powerful as a group of ordinary citizens working together to create change.	SA Explain:	A	D	SD
5. Laws, more than any individual, have the power to change society.	SA Explain:	A	D	SD
6. Because they can't vote, youth have little power to change society.	SA Explain:	A	D	SD
7. While in a democracy "the people" are supposed to have power, in reality most people are powerless to change society. Only elected officials have the power to change society.	SA Explain:	A	D	SD

STRATEGY 2. Dissecting the Prompt

WRITING FOCUS: Understand the writing prompt.

COMMON CORE ALIGNMENT: Write arguments focused on discipline-specific content. (WHST.9-10.1)

RATIONALE

Students need time both to understand what they are being asked to write about and to practice writing about a topic to learn what they think. Dissecting a prompt gives them experience with both the thinking and the decoding of a prompt. Understanding the prompt is the first step in writing a formal essay. Included in each prompt is an overarching essential question that can be used throughout and beyond the unit of study. If you choose to use the essential question, we suggest starting with that and then transitioning into the specific prompt. Otherwise, do the activity below with the specific writing prompt.

PROCEDURE

1. Print out the prompt or the essential question in a larger font and tape it to the center of a piece of paper.

2. Ask students, in pairs, to dissect the prompt. As they read the prompt, direct them to make the following notations:

   - Circle words you do not know or understand in the context of the prompt.
   - Star words that seem to be the central ideas of the prompt.
   - Underline all of the verbs that represent what you, the writer, are supposed to do.
   - Cross out any extra information that does not seem specifically relevant to the writing task.

3. Next, ask students to do a Think-Pair-Share with the prompt. Visit www.facinghistory.org/prompts-strategies/links for more information about this teaching strategy. Individually, students should try to answer the prompt or essential question simply based on their "gut reaction" or personal philosophy. If possible, ask students to try to support their current thinking with an example from history or their own life. After a few minutes, ask each pair to share their thinking with each other. Finally, ask students to share a few opinions or ideas with the larger group.

4. Before moving on, ask students to write the essential question and/or the writing prompt in their interactive notebooks. As they have new thoughts about the prompt throughout the unit, they can make notes to themselves.

STRATEGY 3. Defining Key Terms

WRITING FOCUS: Clarify important vocabulary in the context of the prompt and the history.

COMMON CORE ALIGNMENT: Write arguments about discipline-specific content. (WHST.9-10.1)

RATIONALE

In all the prompts, the way a student defines key terms will determine his or her opinion. In an argumentative essay, word choice and definition are highly important in creating a clear and cohesive argument. The quality of students' essays will depend on how well they understand both the prompt in its entirety and the key vocabulary within the prompt. When writing an argumentative essay in particular, students need to individually decide how they are defining key terms.

PROCEDURE

1. Have students review the words they starred in the Dissecting the Prompt activity. Ask students to write their own definition for each of the starred words.

2. Use **Reproducibles 3.1**, **3.2**, **3.3**, **3.4**, **3.5**, and **3.6** to help students interact with the key words more deeply. For each prompt, the reproducibles focus on different terms specific to the prompt.

3. After completing the two activities, ask students to revisit their first definitions. Has anything changed? Tell students that their current definition is a *working definition* for the unit. It is possible that they will alter their definitions of key terms as they study the history of the civil rights movement.

REPRODUCIBLE 3.1 for Prompt #1

What is injustice?

1. Identify a time when you or someone you know or learned about was treated **unfairly**. Describe the event:

2. Identify a time when you or someone you know or learned about was treated **unjustly**. Describe the event:

3. What is the difference between something that is unfair and something that is unjust?

4. Share examples of injustice with members of your group. Organize examples from least unjust to most unjust (1 = least unjust, 5 = most unjust).

← ——————————————————————————————— →
Least unjust   **Most unjust**
1   2   3   4   5

5. Create a working definition for injustice.

Injustice is....

REPRODUCIBLE 3.2 for Prompt #2

"Strategies" to combat injustice

1. What is a strategy? What does the word "strategy" make you think of?

2. List five "strategies" for being a successful student.

3. List five "strategies" for becoming a famous music star.

4. List five "strategies" for combating injustice.

5. Identify an injustice in your community. (*You might use* **Reproducible 3.1** *to remind yourself of your definition of injustice.*) The injustice can be local, national, or global. Which strategy would you use to challenge this injustice? Why?

   Injustice:

   Strategy:

   Justification (Why do think this strategy would be effective?):

REPRODUCIBLE 3.3 for Prompt #2

What is power?

Step 1: Brainstorm at least five ways to complete the statement "Power is…"

Step 2: To what extent do you agree with these ideas about power? Rank each statement from 1 to 5.

Power is the ability to accomplish your goals.

← ——————————————————————— →
| **Strongly agree** | | | | **Strongly disagree** |
| 1 | 2 | 3 | 4 | 5 |

Power is physical force.

← ——————————————————————— →
| **Strongly agree** | | | | **Strongly disagree** |
| 1 | 2 | 3 | 4 | 5 |

Power is wealth—having the resources that allow you to get things done.

← ——————————————————————— →
| **Strongly agree** | | | | **Strongly disagree** |
| 1 | 2 | 3 | 4 | 5 |

Power is authority—having a position that allows you to tell people what to do.

← ——————————————————————— →
| **Strongly agree** | | | | **Strongly disagree** |
| 1 | 2 | 3 | 4 | 5 |

Power is influence—being able to change a person's behavior.

← ——————————————————————— →
| **Strongly agree** | | | | **Strongly disagree** |
| 1 | 2 | 3 | 4 | 5 |

Step 3: Define "power" in your own words.

Power is…

REPRODUCIBLE 3.4 for Prompt #2

What is social change?

1. In your opinion, what does the word "society" mean?

2. Look up the word "society" in the dictionary. What definition did you find? How does it change the definition you wrote above?

3. Make an identity chart for the word "society" based on your ideas, your classmates' ideas, and the ideas you found in the dictionary.

(society)

4. When we talk about social change, we often talk about events that "change society." Based on your working definition of "society," put an X by the events below that you think have changed or would change society.

   ☐ Facebook is invented.

   ☐ A national law changes the voting age from 21 to 18.

   ☐ A new school policy in New York City bans cell phone use.

   ☐ An enormous hurricane, like Hurricane Katrina, devastates a city on the coast of the United States.

   ☐ Nelson Mandela is elected president of South Africa.

   ☐ In a town that is known for being intolerant to immigrants, Laura Reynolds invites recent immigrants Gloria Garcia and Ang Lee over to her house for dinner.

   ☐ Massachusetts requires students to pass the science MCAS test in order to graduate.

   ☐ College presidents around the country decide to waive tuition payments, making college affordable for virtually all students.

   ☐ France outlaws the wearing of headscarves in public schools.

   ☐ A group of middle-school students work together to successfully reduce bullying at their school.

5. List three criteria you would use to evaluate whether an event changed society. (For example, does an event have to affect more than one person to change society? Does it have to be public? Should you be able to point to a concrete difference in society before and after the event?)

REPRODUCIBLE 3.5 **for Prompt #3**

What is changing the world?

1. Put an X by the events that you think have changed or would change the world.

    ☐ Facebook is invented.

    ☐ A national law changes the voting age from 21 to 18.

    ☐ A new school policy in New York City bans cell phone use.

    ☐ An enormous hurricane, like Hurricane Katrina, devastates a city on the coast of the United States.

    ☐ Nelson Mandela is elected president of South Africa.

    ☐ In a town that is known for being intolerant to immigrants, Laura Reynolds invites recent immigrants Gloria Garcia and Ang Lee over to her house for dinner.

    ☐ Massachusetts requires students to pass the science MCAS test in order to graduate.

    ☐ College presidents around the country decide to waive tuition payments, making college affordable for virtually all students.

    ☐ France outlaws the wearing of headscarves in public schools.

    ☐ A group of middle-school students work together to successfully reduce bullying at their school.

2. List three criteria you would use to evaluate whether an event changed the world. (For example, does an event have to affect more than one person to change the world? Does it have to be public? Should you be able to point to a concrete difference in the world before and after the event?)

REPRODUCIBLE 3.6 for Prompt #3

What constitutes "a small group of committed citizens"?

Step 1: To what extent do you agree with these ideas? Rank each statement from 1 to 5.

A small group of citizens is always less than one hundred people.

← ——————————————————————————— →
Strongly agree   **Strongly disagree**
1   2   3   4   5

A good example of a small group of committed citizens is a club organized at my school.

← ——————————————————————————— →
Strongly agree   **Strongly disagree**
1   2   3   4   5

To be a small group of committed citizens, you need to be organized and intentional.

← ——————————————————————————— →
Strongly agree   **Strongly disagree**
1   2   3   4   5

A small group of committed citizens can be anything from a family marching in a rally to people across the nation voting for the same president.

← ——————————————————————————— →
Strongly agree   **Strongly disagree**
1   2   3   4   5

The Supreme Court is not a small group of committed citizens.

← ——————————————————————————— →
Strongly agree   **Strongly disagree**
1   2   3   4   5

Step 2: Define "a small group of committed citizens" in your own words.

A small group of committed citizens is…

STRATEGY 4. Journal Suggestions

WRITING FOCUS: Students need multiple opportunities and angles to think about and explore a topic before writing a formal essay.

COMMON CORE ALIGNMENT: Write routinely over extended time frames (time for research, reflection, and revisions) and shorter time frames (a single sitting or a day or two) for a range of discipline-specific tasks, purposes, and audiences. (WHST.9-10.10)

RATIONALE

The act of writing helps us figure out what we think. Journaling is one of the most natural ways for students to learn more about themselves as thinkers, writers, and historians. By writing in a journal, students have many opportunities to try out their thinking. As you move through the unit, giving students the opportunity to reflect and practice their thinking will help students generate stronger opinions and ideas when they begin formal writing.

PROCEDURE

Use the following journal prompts during a class period or as homework. We recommend using at least two per week for the duration of the unit.

1. Start by journaling about the essential question for each prompt. Several times throughout the unit, revisit the essential question and ask students to think about how their ideas have changed, grown, or remained consistent.

2. Specific journal entries for each prompt:

    For Prompt #1:

    - Ask students to identify an example of something that is unfair and something that is unjust. It could be something that is happening in their neighborhood, country, or in the world. What is the difference between the two?

    - Why do people have different ideas about injustice? How do we learn what injustice is?

    - Which strategies have people used to fight injustice throughout history? Which have been most effective? How do you know?

    - What do you already know about the history of the civil rights movement? What do you expect to learn about challenging injustice from studying the civil rights movement? What do you already know about this history? What do you want to know?

    - If you had a friend who was trying to right a wrong in their community, what advice would you give him or her? What strategies might you suggest?

    - What does it mean to be someone who stands up against injustice? What is an upstander?

For Prompt #2:

- What does it mean to change society? Does the change have to affect many people? Could someone change society by influencing the people in his/her classroom? In his/her neighborhood?

- Think of a time when something in your community or society changed. What brought about this change? How did the change happen?

- Think of an example of a person in history who was powerful. Why do you think that person had power? Is power always visible?

- What is the relationship between an individual and society? Does society create the individual or does the individual create society?

For Prompt #3:

- Recall a time or incident when a group of people "changed the world." What happened? How do you know they "changed the world"?

- Think of the story of *The Bear That Wasn't* (see www.facinghistory.org/prompts-strategies/links to watch a video of this story). Was the bear changed by society? How do you know?

- What else (besides a group of thoughtful committed citizens) can change the world?

- Is changing the world always good? Can change ever be negative? Use examples from history and current events to answer this question.

- What does it mean to change the world? Does the change have to affect many people? Could someone change the world by influencing the people in his/her classroom? In his/her neighborhood?

- Think of a time when something in your community or family changed. What brought about this change? How did the change happen?

STRATEGIES TO USE DURING THE STUDY OF *CIVIL RIGHTS HISTORICAL INVESTIGATIONS*

B. GATHERING AND ANALYZING EVIDENCE

*Use these strategies **during** the unit.*

Once students understand the prompt and have begun to form opinions on the broad issues, they are ready to dig into the historical content. The strategies in this section help students think about *what* they are reading and learning. Historical reasoning requires students to focus on evidence, perspective, and interpretation.[1] By closely investigating a wide variety of primary and secondary sources, students begin to develop their own arguments.

One of the challenges in supporting students-as-writers and students-as-historians is in helping them understand how to work with evidence. Specifically, they need practice offering accurate and persuasive evidence, considering the source and credibility of the evidence, and citing sufficient and contextualized evidence that demonstrates their understanding of the historical period.[2]

These activities help students engage with the evidence, and they *precede* the work of actually synthesizing the evidence and crafting a thesis statement. Students are not yet expected to begin their formal essay. The purpose of this section is to have students thinking critically about the relationship between the historical content in the *Civil Rights Historical Investigations* unit and the CWA prompt.

This section includes both written and oral strategies. Discussions let students build their own understanding and "rehearse" their thinking before writing[3]; even the strongest students are challenged to revise and refine their thinking when their peers offer opposing views. Discussions also let teachers listen in to gauge how well the group or specific individuals understand the content, in order to provide clarification or differentiated support as needed.

---

[1] Chauncey Monte-Sano, "Beyond Reading Comprehension and Summary: Learning to Read and Write in History by Focusing on Evidence, Perspective, and Interpretation," *Curriculum Inquiry* 41, no. 2 (2011): 212–249.

[2] Chauncey Monte-Sano, "Disciplinary Literacy in History: An Exploration of the Historical Nature of Adolescents' Writing," *Journal of the Learning Sciences* 19, no. 4 (2010): 539–568.

[3] Martin Nystrand, Adam Gamoran, and William Carbonaro, "Towards an Ecology or Learning: The Case of Classroom Discourse and Its Effects on Writing in High School English and Social Studies" (Center on English Learning & Achievement, Report Number 11001, 1998), accessed October 22, 2011, http://www.albany.edu/cela/reports/nystrand/nystrandtowards11001.pdf.

STRATEGY 5. Evidence Logs and Index Cards

WRITING FOCUS: Students collect evidence to defend their argument.

COMMON CORE ALIGNMENT: Draw evidence from informational texts to support analysis, reflection, and research. (WHST.9-10.9)

RATIONALE

Students need a central place to organize and revisit the textual evidence they collect. This will help them to create a clear and coherent thesis. As students study history, they will interrogate primary sources to find evidence to answer at least one of the prompts. Collecting evidence will allow students to weigh the possible sides of the argument and eventually craft a thesis that they are able to defend. Having the evidence in a central location or structure helps students review the history and pick clear and relevant reasons to support their thinking.

PROCEDURE

1. Introduce one or several of the evidence logs to your class before you start studying the history. Explain that as you study different documents and watch different historical footage, students will record textual evidence to use in their formal essays. Explain that the goal throughout the unit is to collect evidence from multiple perspectives and keep it in their interactive notebooks to use throughout the unit. Students will then later review the variety of evidence and use it both to determine and support their argument.

2. As they collect evidence, make sure that students are recording the details of each primary or secondary source. Model for students the type of information they need to include about each source (author, title, publisher, date, page, type of source). You might want to keep a poster on the wall to remind students or give them a handout they can tape into their notebooks. Helpful resources for you and students include (both of these sites post information about MLA and APA styles):

   - Cornell Library Citation Management Page (visit www.facinghistory.org/prompts-strategies/links for a link to the page)
   - Purdue Online Writing Lab (OWL): Research and Citation (visit www.facinghistory.org/prompts-strategies/links for a link to the page)

Note: Included in this section are two evidence logs specific to each prompt and one generic evidence log that can be used with any prompt. We anticipate and hope that you will modify, adapt, and create evidence logs to best fit the needs of your particular students and classroom context.

REPRODUCIBLE 5.1 Evidence Log for Prompt #1

Strategy: _____

Directions: Identify three examples of when this strategy was used. Then complete the chart with information about this example.

	Example 1	Example 2	Example 3
Where and when was this strategy used?			
Why? For what purpose?			
By whom?			
Consequences: In this instance, how did this strategy challenge injustice?			
Consequences: In this instance, how did this strategy hinder the struggle against injustice?			
Source/s and quality of source (1-3)			

facinghistory.org

REPRODUCIBLE 5.2 Index cards for Prompt #1

Front of card:

Which strategy was used?	
Where?	
When?	
Why? What injustice was being responded to?	
By whom?	
Consequences	
How did the use of this strategy **help** the struggle against injustice?	How did the use of this strategy **hinder** the struggle against injustice?

Back of card:

<u>Source</u>

Citation:

Quality of source (1-3):

Why did you give it this ranking?

REPRODUCIBLE 5.3 Evidence Log for Prompt #2

Which statement does the history of the civil rights movement most support?

A. An individual is powerless to change society.

B. An individual has the power to change society.

Source #	Relevant information (Who or what was trying to change society? How? When? Where? Was the effort successful?)	Which statement does this evidence support? A? B? Both? Explain.

REPRODUCIBLE 5.4 Index card for Prompt #2

Front of card contains information such as:

> **Who** was trying to change society?
>
> **What** was he/she/they/it doing to change society?
>
> **When** and **where** did this occur?
>
> **How** did it work out? Successful? Unsuccessful?
>
> Evaluate which statement this evidence supports (1-5): _____
>
> ← ─── →
>
> 1   2   3   4   5
>
> **An individual is powerless to change society.**   **An individual has the power to change society.**

Back of card contains information about the source such as:

> <u>Source</u>
>
> Citation:
>
>
>
> Quality of source (1-3):
>
> Why did you give it this ranking?

REPRODUCIBLE 5.5 Evidence Log #1 for Prompt #3

Key for labels:

A. "Concerned group of thoughtful, committed citizens"
B. Elected official
C. Judge (judicial system)
D. Individual
E. Global events (events happening around the world)
F. Media
G. Public opinion
H. Natural disaster
I. Other:
J. Other:

Change agent	Label	What did he/she/they/it do to change the world?	Source information (document name, who said it, date...)	Comments and questions
Link	Individual	He helped Melba escape from the kids who were trying to hurt her.	*Warriors Don't Cry* by Melba Pattillo Beals (171–172)	How did this impact the situation beyond Melba? Why would he do this?

REPRODUCIBLE 5.6 Evidence Log #2 for Prompt #3

Change agent	Examples	What did they do to change the world during the civil rights movement?	Sources – Where did you find this information?
Concerned group of thoughtful committed citizens	1. Little Rock 9		
	2. NAACP		
Elected officials (leaders)			
Courts (justice system)			
Media			
Individuals			
Other:			
Other:			

40 FACING HISTORY & OURSELVES

REPRODUCIBLE 5.7 **Evidence Log: Generic**

CWA Prompt:

Doc #	Citation	Summary — What information from this source addresses the CWA prompt?	Information about author/creator	Source rank (1–3)
1				
2				
3				

STRATEGY 6. Annotating and Paraphrasing Sources

WRITING FOCUS: Students learn to search and annotate texts for evidence.

COMMON CORE ALIGNMENT:. Gather relevant information from multiple authoritative print and digital sources, using advanced searches effectively; assess the usefulness of each source in answering the research question; integrate information into the text selectively to maintain the flow of ideas, avoiding plagiarism and following a standard format for citation. (WHST.9-10.8)

Draw evidence from literary or informational texts to support analysis, reflection, and research. (WHST.9-10.9)

RATIONALE

In order to craft strong arguments about historical events, students need to understand primary and secondary source documents. Careful reading is integral to powerful writing. Annotating text—by underlining key words or writing notes, questions, and margin notes to oneself—often helps students with this close and careful reading. This careful structured reading, in turn, has been found to lead to improved writing.[4] Students learn to make notes that address the validity and bias of evidence, the perspective of the source, and their own interpretation.[5]

PROCEDURE

Note: Annotating can and should occur throughout the unit. Below is a procedure you might use to introduce the purpose of annotating and to get started. Students will need regular practice, reinforcement, and feedback on their annotations in order for this type of careful reading to become routine.

1. Show students sample annotations—your own or from other students.

    - Ask students what they see.

2. Ask students why they think historians annotate as they read. Discuss the value of the following:

    - a way of "talking to the text"[6] and having a dialogue with yourself[7] as you read

    - a way to slow down your thinking as you read hard text, so you read more closely, "thoughtfully, mindfully, intentionally"[8]

    - an opportunity to sort out the material: what you understand and what is still puzzling[9]

---

[4] Monte-Sano, "Beyond Reading Comprehension," 224.
[5] Ibid.
[6] Shoenbach, 1999, as found in Monte-Sano, *Curriculum Inquiry*, 238.
[7] Case study teacher in Monte-Sano, "Beyond Reading Comprehension," 225.
[8] Case study teacher in Monte-Sano, "Beyond Reading Comprehension." Pseudonym of teacher is Lyle; real name not given.
[9] Ibid.

- a way to keep track of your thinking as you read so you can revisit and use that thinking later when you are debating or when you are writing your essay

3. Model annotating a short primary source document in front of the class. Be sure you model both simple summarizing/paraphrasing and more complex critical thinking as you read. Options:
   - Circle or underline key words; tell students why these seem important.
   - Put a question mark by ideas you don't understand or find puzzling.
   - Summarize key historical events and ideas: Does this make sense? What does this say? What does this mean?
   - Write phrases or sentences that express your reactions and interpretations.
   - Note the author's intentions and assumptions.

4. Give students a short text to annotate on their own or in small groups.
   - Circulate to give them feedback on their annotations.
   - After they have read and annotated, have students compare their annotations.
     » What did you write?
     » How did it help you?
     » How were your peers' annotations different?

5. Ask students to annotate throughout the unit.
   - Periodically remind them of the essential question and writing prompt as a way to help them focus their thinking as they read. What should they be paying attention to?
   - Check their annotations.
   - Give students feedback. Write your own thinking back to them or talk with students about their margin notes. What strikes you? What ideas seem worth pursuing?
   - Remind students that they should use these margin notes when they write their essays.

VARIATION

Students annotate electronically using online tools or software.

STRATEGY 7. Collecting and Sharing Evidence

WRITING FOCUS: Find additional evidence from historical documents and peers to support an argument.

COMMON CORE ALIGNMENT: Gather relevant information from multiple print and digital sources. (WHST.9-10.8)

Develop claim(s) and counterclaims fairly, supplying data and evidence for each while pointing out the strengths and limitations of both claim(s) and counterclaims in a discipline-appropriate form and in a manner that anticipates the audience's knowledge level and concerns. (WHST.9-101b)

Initiate and participate effectively in a range of collaborative discussions (one-on-one, in groups, and teacher-led) with diverse partners on grades 9–10 topics, texts, and issues, building on others' ideas and expressing their own clearly and persuasively. (SL.9-10.1)

RATIONALE

Students need to interrogate and investigate multiple primary sources and ideas to stimulate their thinking and find evidence for their argument. Teachers can also use these strategies as a way to have students share their work with peers. Students will practice being active listeners or readers—an essential skill for learning new information.

Below are three possible strategies: Gallery Walk; Give One, Get One; and Two-Minute Interview. Choose the one that best suits your students and classroom.

A. Gallery Walk

PROCEDURE

1. **Preparation.** Start by organizing primary source documents around the classroom, either on walls or placed on tables. The most important factor is that the texts are spread far enough apart to reduce significant crowding.

2. **Instruct Students on How to Walk Through the Gallery.** You might want them to take informal notes, use a graphic organizer, or create an evidence bank as they view the "gallery." You may also want them to interact with the documents by writing questions, defining terms, or adding information to a document.

3. **Debriefing the Gallery Walk and Journal Writing.** Spend some time reviewing what students posted and recorded to make sure information is accurate. It is also important to give students the opportunity to ask questions about items in the Gallery Walk that may be confusing.

B. Give One, Get One

PROCEDURE

1. **Preparation.** Ask students to divide a sheet of paper into two vertical columns. Label the left side "Give One" and the right side "Get One."

2. **Response to the Question.** Ask students to respond to a question such as "How did the media and the invention of the television impact the civil rights movement?" or "Do you think young people can change the world? Why or why not?" Students should write their ideas on the left-hand column on their paper. They do not need to write complete sentences; responses can be in list form.

3. **Give One, Get One.** Tell students to walk around and find a partner. Each partner "gives," or shares, items from his or her list. For example, Partner A shares his/her responses until Partner B hears something that is not already on his/her list. Partner B writes the new response in the right column on the paper, along with Partner A's name. Once Partner B has "gotten" one, the roles switch. Students repeat this process with other peers until time runs out.

C. Two-Minute Interview

PROCEDURE

1. **Preparation.** Ask students to create a list of questions they have about the historical case study or the evidence they have collected. Alternatively, you can ask students to respond to a question such as "How did the media and the invention of the television impact the civil rights movement?" or "Do you think young people can change the world? Why or why not?" (Use **Reproducible 7.1** to help students organize their thinking during this activity.)

2. **Two-Minute Interviews.**

    a. Divide the class in half randomly. Place chairs in two long rows, facing each other. Students will sit facing each other.

    b. Tell students that they will have two minutes to interview each other. One row of students will ask the questions, listen carefully, and take notes. The other row will answer.

    c. After two minutes, have one row of students move down so that everyone has a new partner to share evidence or ideas with. Continue this activity until you feel that students have gathered enough evidence or shared enough ideas to generate a full-class discussion.

Debriefing All Three Strategies

After each of these strategies, you will want to debrief in a class discussion and/or a journal write. See guidelines for discussion in the box below.

Prompts for journal writing include:

- How might you respond to the essay prompt now?
- What did you learn today? How does this information relate to the essay prompt?
- What else do you want to know?

> ### Teacher's role:
>
> As the students share their ideas, keep notes. Pay particular attention to:
>
> - patterns of insight, understanding, or strong historical reasoning
> - patterns of confusion, historical inaccuracies, or facile connections, or thinking that indicates students are making overly simplified comparisons between past and present
>
> The goal is for students to share text-based evidence effectively and accurately. The following categories can guide you, the teacher, as you listen to your students' discussion. Listen for:
>
> - **Factual and interpretive accuracy:** offering evidence that is correct and interpretations that are plausible
> - **Persuasiveness of evidence:** including evidence that is relevant and strong in terms of helping to prove the claim
> - **Sourcing of evidence:** noting what the source is and its credibility and/or bias
> - **Corroboration of evidence:** recognizing how different documents work together to support a claim
> - **Contextualization of evidence:** placing the evidence into its appropriate historical context[10]
>
> As students debrief, weave in feedback. Affirm their insights. Highlight strong historical reasoning and text-based arguments. Choose one or two misconceptions about the content to address. Point out areas where students may want to reevaluate the ways they are connecting past and present.

---

10 Monte-Sano, "Beyond Reading Comprehension."

REPRODUCIBLE 7.1 Two-Minute Interviews

Question I asked	Person I interviewed	Notes/thoughts/new questions that I now have
Do you think the music of the civil rights movement was a strategy that helped defeat injustice? Why or why not?	Jacob	Maybe the music helped people keep their focus…remember the "Freedom Riders" clip about how the music helped them get through jail without being frustrated or using violence…

facinghistory.org

STRATEGY 8. Evaluating Evidence

WRITING FOCUS: Students will sort and sift through evidence to prepare to write their essays.

COMMON CORE ALIGNMENT: Draw evidence from informational texts to support analysis, reflection, and research. (WHST.9-10.9)

RATIONALE

Students need to be able to evaluate evidence in order to craft a strong argument. Scholars focused on historical reasoning note that evidence-based interpretations are central to the discipline.[11] Historians must be able to source evidence (noting author's intentions, assumptions, and motivations), contextualize evidence (situating a historical document in the time and place in which it was created), and corroborate evidence (comparing multiple historical documents to help one make sense and determine acceptable facts).[12] They must also determine what evidence is most persuasive and how to account for evidence that conflicts with their central claim. The strategy below is a hands-on way to get students to begin to sort and sift evidence, determining what it means and why it matters.

PROCEDURE

1. In advance:
   - Draft a claim that the class will work with. It could be an answer to one of the prompts, or it could be some other claim related to the unit that is independent of the specific formal writing prompts. Things to keep in mind include:
     a. It must be arguable: something that could be true but isn't necessarily true.
     b. It must be a claim that requires students to grapple with evidence.
   - Gather a variety of evidence from the Facing History unit: texts, photographs, primary sources, etc. Include:
     a. some evidence that could be used to help prove the claim
     b. some evidence that could be used to help disprove the claim
     c. some evidence that could be used either way, depending on the interpretation
     d. some evidence that is simply irrelevant to the claim

Note: If you choose to use their evidence logs, try to photocopy them before the class so that students can cut each piece of evidence onto a separate strip of paper. The physical act of manipulating evidence is key to the effectiveness of this activity.

---

[11] Ibid., 236.
[12] Wineburg as found in Monte-Sano, *Curriculum Inquiry*, 13.

2. In class:
   - As you begin this activity with students, explain some things that historians consider when working with evidence:

     Factual accuracy: How do we know the evidence is correct?

     Relevance: To what extent does this evidence relate to the topic/question at hand?

     Persuasiveness: Is this evidence powerful in convincing us of the claim?

     Source: Where does the evidence come from? How credible is the source? What biases exist?

   - On the board, write the claim the class will work with.
   - Distribute the collected evidence to table groups or ask them to take out their evidence logs.
   - Invite them to "sort and sift" the evidence they might use to help prove the claim. Different table groups may sort and sift differently, which is appropriate. They could organize the evidence by what proves and disproves the claim, by what is relevant or irrelevant to the activity, etc. The goal is for students to be able to justify/explain the decisions they make.
   - After the task, debrief the activity using some of the following prompts:
     a. How has this activity helped them think about this specific evidence?
     b. What did they learn by doing this activity that they might apply when choosing and analyzing evidence in their own argumentative writing?
     c. Reiterate the criteria historians tend to use when working with evidence:
        » accuracy
        » relevance
        » persuasiveness
        » source

3. After the activity and throughout the rest of this unit, have students evaluate the evidence they collect by going through this sorting and sifting activity. Remind students that their essays will be much stronger if they choose strong, specific, and appropriate evidence to defend their claims.

STRATEGY 9. Relevant or Not?

WRITING FOCUS: Using this strategy, students will be able to distinguish between evidence that is relevant to support an argument and evidence that is not relevant to support an argument.

COMMON CORE ALIGNMENT: Introduce precise claim(s), distinguish the claim(s) from alternate or opposing claims, and create an organization that establishes clear relationships among the claim(s), counterclaims, reasons, and evidence. (WHST.9-10.1a)

RATIONALE

After students collect evidence, they need to evaluate which evidence best suits their needs. One important step in learning how to support an argument (in speaking or writing) is determining which evidence to use. The purpose of this strategy is to help students distinguish between relevant and irrelevant evidence so that they can make appropriate selections for their essays.

PROCEDURE

1. MODELING. In this exercise, students will identify evidence that is relevant to prove a particular claim. This activity is most effective if students have a basic command of the concept of relevance. Therefore, we suggest modeling this process with a few examples. You can start with a non-history-based example like this one and then test students' understanding on a history-based example.

Examples

Claim: *Cell phones should not be allowed in school.*

Which of the following pieces of evidence address the above claim?

a. Cell phones distract from the learning environment. Students who text or play games on their phones during class do not hear directions or miss learning important content.

b. Many students today bring cell phones to school.

c. Cell phones are more affordable now than they were in 2000.

d. In surveys, some students report using their cell phones to cheat on exams.

Ask students which of the four pieces of evidence are *not* relevant to proving this claim. Here are some ideas to bring up during a discussion of this question:

- "a" and "d" are both relevant to the claim.
- "b" provides accurate information but is irrelevant to proving the claim.
- "c" may or may not be accurate. It is also irrelevant to the claim.

Historical claim: The civil rights movement demonstrates that the strategy of nonviolence is an effective way to challenge injustice.

Which of the following evidence addresses the above argument?

a. Challenging injustice was one of the goals of the civil rights movement.

b. During Freedom Summer, protesters used nonviolent methods to help Black Americans register to vote.

c. On March 7, marchers in Selma organized a nonviolent march to Montgomery to protest against voter discrimination against African Americans. Even when the protesters were fired at with tear gas and were beaten with batons, they did not retaliate with violence. This strategy effectively gained sympathy from the American public for their cause, motivating President Johnson to submit Voting Rights legislation to Congress one week later. (*Eyes on the Prize*, "Bridge to Freedom")

d. "This method was made famous in our generation by Mohandas K. Gandhi, who used it to free India form the domination of the British empire."(Martin Luther King, Jr. in the article "Nonviolence and Racial Justice," 1957)

Ask students which of the four pieces of evidence is NOT relevant to proving this argument. Here are some ideas that you might bring up during a discussion of this question:

- While "a" may be correct, it is not relevant to proving the argument. This is the kind of statement that might go into the introduction, however.

- "b" could be used, but is not sufficient on its own. The statement is accurate but it does not prove how nonviolence was effective at challenging an injustice (e.g. expanding voting rights for African Americans).

- "c" exemplifies relevant evidence: it describes an example of nonviolence and then explains how it helps effectively combat an injustice during the civil rights movement (e.g. voter discrimination).

- "d" provides an example of when nonviolence helped confront injustice, but it is an example from India.

2. GROUP WORK. Continue to have students practice this exercise individually or in groups. Provide historical claims for students, and have each individual or group come up with three pieces of evidence that might be used to support the claim. Two of these selections should represent relevant evidence—evidence that addresses the particular argument. One of these selections should be accurate and credible but not relevant to proving that particular argument. Explain to students that they will present their argument and three pieces of evidence to the whole class (or to another group) and that the audience will have to determine which evidence is relevant and which is irrelevant.

STRATEGY 10. Learning to Infer

WRITING FOCUS: Infer from primary and secondary sources.

COMMON CORE ALIGNMENT: Draw evidence from informational texts to support analysis, reflection, and research. (WHST.9-10.9)

RATIONALE

Inference requires students to take something from the text, combine it with some existing background knowledge, and make a new connection. Show them how you do this as a more expert historian. In order to write convincingly about primary and secondary source documents, students must first be able to interpret those documents. Students need support in moving beyond the literal meaning in the texts to making inferences about significance. Teaching students how historians infer, naming that process for them, and giving them opportunities to practice inferring orally will help prepare them to transfer that skill to their written historical analysis.

This strategy is more inquiry-based, allowing students to first make inferences and then learn the formal concept of inference. Research indicates that both authentic inquiry and explicit instruction help students as writers. Be sure you balance out this inquiry strategy with some of the strategies in this same section that offer more explicit instruction.

PROCEDURE

1. Give students a real-world scenario that requires them to infer. (Do not name inference yet for your students.) For example, share a tidbit of gossip or something from a current event.

2. Using that real-world example, name what they did when they inferred. Ask:
   - What was the text or data?
   - What was their background knowledge?
   - How do they automatically put the two together for the "aha" that is inference?

3. Model how you infer as a historian.
   - Read or write up some data.
   - Tell them your background knowledge.
   - Show them how you put the two together to make an inference or interpretation.

The options below show two specific scaffolds to teach students how to infer. Choose one to use with your students.

OPTION A:

It says . . . I say . . . And so . . . [13]

It says . . . (the text or data)	I say . . . (my background knowledge)	And so . . . (put the two together to make an inference)
The chaos in Little Rock during the desegregation of Central High School was covered in newspapers around the world.	The United States likes to maintain good relationships with other countries and be a leader in the world.	President Eisenhower might be embarrassed by the media, which will affect how he chooses to act during the crisis.

OPTION B: INFERENCE EQUATION [14]

I notice + I already know = So now I am thinking . . .

I notice

　that the crisis in Little Rock is being covered in media around the world.

+ I already know

　that the United States likes to maintain good relationships with other countries and be a leader in the world.

= So now I am thinking

　that President Eisenhower might be embarrassed by the media, which will affect how he handles the crisis in Little Rock.

I notice . . .

+ I already know . . .

= So now I am thinking . . .

---

13 Kyleen Beers, *When Kids Can't Read: What Teachers Can Do* (Heinemann, 2003).

14 Inference equation developed by Nicole Frazier, former social studies teacher at Manual High School, Denver Public Schools, Denver, CO, 2008.

STRATEGY 11. Assessing Source Credibility

WRITING FOCUS: Students practice media literacy by determining which sources they can trust for credible, accurate, and persuasive evidence.

COMMON CORE ALIGNMENT: Gather relevant information from multiple authoritative print and digital sources . . . assess the usefulness of each source. (WHST.9-10.8)

RATIONALE

Especially now that students have access to a limitless amount of information posted on the Internet, it is critical that they develop strong media literacy skills. As students gather information, they need to evaluate the credibility of their sources. What perspective does this source represent? Why should this source be trusted? What makes this source more or less credible than other sources? Resources that provide additional information about source evaluation include:

- Project Look Sharp.
- Purdue Online Writing Lab (OWL): Evaluating Sources of Information.

PROCEDURE

1. **Brainstorm.** Students may not be aware of how often they practice evaluating sources. For example, they might hear a rumor and know not to believe the information. You can begin this exercise by asking students to respond to the question: How do you decide when to trust what you see, hear, or read? Record a list on the board of criteria they use or steps they take to determine if a source is credible.

2. **Create a Checklist.** Based on students' responses and your additional ideas, create a checklist students can use to determine if a source is trustworthy. Items on the checklist might include:

   - Information can be backed up by another source or sources.
   - Author/creator is an expert on the topic.
   - Author/creator experienced the situation firsthand.
   - Information is published by a credible institution (a business that could get into a lot of trouble if it printed inaccurate information), such as a major newspaper, PBS, Library of Congress, a major museum, etc.

You can also make a checklist for possible reasons not to trust a source, such as:

- It has an anonymous author or creator and there is no way to determine if the author is an expert on this subject.
- Information is not published by an organization; it's unclear who else stands by this information.

- Information in this source contradicts much of the information you have read elsewhere.
- No references are provided for this information; there's no way to find out if this information is true or false.

3. **Group Work.** Pass out documents and have groups or pairs evaluate the same source or sources and then compare their rankings. You might use the sample source evaluation form (**Reproducible 11.1**).

4. **Individual Work and Assessment.** For homework, you can ask students to find and evaluate a source on their own. Completed source evaluation forms will tell you the degree to which students have mastered this skill.

> You also might wish to have a discussion about the credibility of Wikipedia, a source that many students are quick to use, as it comes up first in many search-engine results. Wikipedia puts neutrality and reliability alerts on some of its pages. Key questions to ask students might be:
>
> - What does the phrase "the neutrality of this article is disputed" mean? Why is that important to think about as you collect evidence?
> - How do you know when you can trust the information on Wikipedia?
> - Where else might you go to verify an idea listed on Wikipedia?

REPRODUCIBLE 11.1 Source Evaluation Form: Why Should You Trust This Source? Why Shouldn't You Trust This Source?

Part 1: Basic Source Information

Author/creator:
Year published/created:
Published by:
Type of source (newspaper, photograph, article, law, etc.):
Other information about this source:

Part 2: Rank the Trustworthiness of This Source: _____

3 = very trustworthy, 2 = trustworthy, 1 = some reservations, 0 = not trustworthy

Checklist

- ☐ Author/creator is an expert on the topic.
- ☐ Author/creator experienced the situation firsthand.
- ☐ Information is backed up by several other sources (includes citations and/or you have seen similar information in other credible sources).
- ☐ Information is published by a credible institution (a business that could get into a lot of trouble if it printed inaccurate information), such as a major newspaper, PBS, Library of Congress, a major museum, etc.

Part 3: Bias/Perspective

What do you know about the author/creator of this source?

What bias or perspective does this source represent? What is the creator in favor of or against?

What are the strengths of this source? What information can the author/creator reliably present? (Examples: A zoologist would be a more reliable source about elephants than a dentist. Someone who has lived in Boston for 50 years may be a more reliable source about the T than someone who has visited Boston once. However, if that Boston resident never rode the T and that visitor rode the T extensively for a whole week, the visitor may be a more reliable source.)

STRATEGY 12. Successful Online Research

WRITING FOCUS: Students analyze and collect evidence to defend their argument.

COMMON CORE ALIGNMENT: Gather relevant information from multiple print and digital sources, using advanced searches effectively; assess the usefulness of each source in answering the research question; integrate information into the text selectively to maintain the flow of ideas, avoiding plagiarism and following a standard format for citation. (WHST.9-10.8)

RATIONALE

Students need to understand how to most effectively search for relevant, trusted information on the Internet. As students study history, they will interrogate primary and secondary sources to find evidence that will allow them to eventually craft a thesis that they are able to defend. Being able to use advanced searching techniques will ensure students are able to access the latest and most useful information.

PROCEDURE

We highly recommend you use the following resource to help you create online research activities in your classroom:

- Teaching History With Technology from EdTech Teacher (visit www.facinghistory.org/prompts-strategies/links for a link to this page). This presents a wealth of information about online research in the history classroom. It includes a list of student-friendly search engines and links to collections of primary sources. In addition, there are video tutorials about advanced Google searches, evaluating source credibility, and creating online bookmarks with students.

- Google Lesson Plans. Google has created lesson plans to help students learn how to search effectively with Google. There are beginner, intermediate, and advanced lessons available.

STRATEGIES TO USE AFTER COMPLETING *CIVIL RIGHTS HISTORICAL INVESTIGATIONS*, WHILE WRITING FORMAL ESSAY

C. CRAFTING A THESIS AND ORGANIZING IDEAS

Use these strategies **after** *the unit.*

Once students have had an opportunity to engage with the evidence, they can begin to integrate, synthesize, and categorize their ideas. In this section, teachers can challenge students to sort out "What is *my* perspective on this issue?"

Much of historical thinking and writing involves forming strong arguments or interpretations based on the core concepts in history: Why does this matter? How did this happen? What motivated people in the past to think and act in the ways they did? How do we know what we know? How was this past situation similar to present-day situations? The prompts are designed to engage students in these big questions.

Note: We placed crafting a thesis *after* students have had many opportunities *throughout* the unit to examine and understand the evidence. A recent study found that college professors express concern that many students leap to writing a thesis before they have explored their ideas in sufficient detail.[1] Here, crafting a thesis and organizing ideas are paired, as a way to help students begin to integrate, synthesize, and categorize their ideas.

---

[1] Stevi Quate, ed., "Lessons Learned: A Report of the DASSC Writing Inquiry Project," June 1, 2011, http://writinginquiry.wikispaces.com/file/view/Lessonslearned.pdf.

STRATEGY 13. Taking a Stand on Controversial Issues: Speaking and Listening Strategies

WRITING FOCUS: Students will practice using evidence to make and defend an argument.

COMMON CORE ALIGNMENT: Develop claim(s) and counterclaims fairly, supplying data and evidence for each while pointing out the strengths and limitations of both claim(s) and counterclaims in a discipline-appropriate form and in a manner that anticipates the audience's knowledge level and concerns. (WHST.9-10.1b)

Initiate and participate effectively in a range of collaborative discussions (one-on-one, in groups, and teacher-led) with diverse partners on grades 9–10 topics, texts, and issues, building on others' ideas and expressing their own clearly and persuasively. (SL.9-10.1)

RATIONALE

Speaking and listening strategies give students early practice with explaining how evidence supports their position. These strategies also support students' critical thinking, since students consider an issue from multiple perspectives. Engaging in speaking and listening can be an effective writing exercise before an essay assignment because it brings out arguments for or against a thesis. It can also be effective after writing a first draft of an essay; often, a classroom discussion will clarify thinking and help a student locate the part of their argument to revise.

Because these strategies involve sharing opinions, often in a passionate way, set a contract before this activity. Reiterate your class rules about respect for the opinions and voices of others; call for them to be honest but not insulting. Readdress ways to constructively disagree with one another, and require that when offering their opinion or defense of their stance, they speak from the "I," rather than from an accusatory "You."

A. Barometer

PROCEDURE

1. **Preparation.** Place "Strongly Agree" and "Strongly Disagree" signs at opposite ends of a continuum in your room. Or you can post any statement and its opposite at two ends of a continuum. Any argument or thesis statement can be used for this activity. Give students a few minutes to respond to the prompt in writing before you ask them to "take a stand."

2. **"Take a Stand."** Ask students to stand on the spot of the line that represents their opinion, telling them that if they stand on either extreme they are absolute in their agreement or disagreement. They may also stand anywhere in between the two extremes, depending on how much they agree or disagree with the statement.

3. **Explain Positions.** Once students have lined up, ask them to explain why they have chosen to stand where they are. Encourage students to refer to evidence and examples when defending their stance. If students are persuaded to change their opinion, ask them to move along the continuum to show their new thinking.

B. SPAR (Spontaneous Argumentation)

PROCEDURE

1. **Preparation.** Divide class in half. Assign one side to be the *pro* position and the other side to be the *con* position. Have students move their desks so they are sitting opposite an opponent. Write a debatable proposition on the board.

2. **Brainstorm Arguments.** Give students one to two minutes to write down their arguments and evidence for or against the proposition.

3. **Opening Statements.** The students will be "SPARring" with the person sitting across from them. Each student (*pro* and *con*) presents a **one-minute opening statement** making his/her case while the other listens quietly and takes notes.

4. **Discussion.** Give students 30 seconds to prepare ideas for what they want to say to their opponent. Invite each side to engage in a **three-minute discussion** during which they may question their opponent's reasoning or examples or put forth new ones of their own.

5. **Closing Statements.** Give students 30 seconds or one minute to prepare a closing statement. *Each* student presents a **one-minute closing statement** while the other listens quietly, and then the roles reverse.

C. Final Word

This strategy is a way for students to talk without having the competitiveness that can accompany debate in the classroom.

PROCEDURE

1. **Preparation.** Divide students into groups of four and have them position themselves so that they are in a circle.

2. **Prompts.** Create a list of claims for students to respond to or ask students to write their own claims (thesis statements).

3. **Sharing in Small Groups.** Ask each group to choose someone to begin. The first few times that you do "Final Word," remind students of the procedure before you officially begin. The first student has 30 seconds to respond to the claim or share his or her thesis statement. After 30 seconds, the person to the right of the first student has a chance to react to the thesis. This student can choose to respond to the first student or simply give his or her own information. After 30 seconds, the third student speaks, following the same rules. Continue the process with the fourth student. After the fourth student, the first student now gets to have the "Final Word." He or she receives an additional 30 seconds to respond to the comments of the group, to argue for his or her point, or to summarize the thoughts of the group. In the next round, a different student should begin.

A FEW NOTES:

- No students should speak when it is not their turn to talk. The goal is for each student to have 30 seconds that are entirely his or hers.
- If a student doesn't talk for his or her entire 30 seconds, the group should wait for the time to run out before the next person begins.

Debrief

After any of these activities, engage your class in a discussion. Questions to ask include:

- What were the arguments for and against the issue?
- What did you learn during the activity? How does this information relate to the essay prompt?
- What value is to be gained from students arguing positions with which they don't agree?
- What were the strongest arguments? Which arguments were the weakest? What role does evidence play in creating an argument?

Teacher's role:

As students share their ideas, keep notes. Pay particular attention to:

- patterns of insight, understanding, or strong historical reasoning
- patterns of confusion, historical inaccuracies, facile connections, or thinking that indicates students are making overly simplified comparisons between past and present

The goal is for students to share text-based evidence effectively and accurately. The following categories can guide you, the teacher, as you listen to your students' discussion. Listen for:

- **Factual and interpretive accuracy:** offering evidence that is correct and interpretations that are plausible
- **Persuasiveness of evidence:** including evidence that is relevant and strong in terms of helping to prove the claim
- **Sourcing of evidence:** noting what the source is and its credibility and/or bias
- **Corroboration of evidence:** recognizing how different documents work together to support a claim
- **Contextualization of evidence:** placing the evidence into its appropriate historical context[2]

As students debrief, weave in feedback. Affirm their insights. Highlight strong historical reasoning and text-based arguments. Choose one or two misconceptions about the content to address. Point out areas where students may want to reevaluate the ways they are connecting past and present.

---

2 Monte-Sano, "Beyond Reading Comprehension."

STRATEGY 14. Building Arguments through Mini-Debates

WRITING FOCUS: Students will practice using evidence to make and defend an argument.

COMMON CORE ALIGNMENT: Support claim(s) with logical reasoning and relevant, accurate data and evidence that demonstrate an understanding of the topic or text, using credible sources. (WHST.9-10.1b)

RATIONALE

This strategy helps students work with two key components of Toulmin's model of argument: claim and evidence. They are not yet being asked to provide analysis or a "warrant" explaining how the evidence proves the claim/reason.

PROCEDURE

1. Create a list of items, with or without your students, that could be used to answer the prompt. For example, if your students are trying to decide what strategies were more effective during the civil rights movement, create a list of strategies.

2. Write each strategy on a separate index card. *(Note: The graphic organizers below use Prompt #1 with this activity; however, you will want to tailor your classroom to the specific prompt your students are trying to answer.)*

3. Divide the class into groups or pairs. Pass out one card to each group. Together, each group is responsible for filling out the accompanying chart for the subject of their card.

4. After each pair or group has filled out its card, hold a mini-debate in the classroom. Pick a card at random and ask the pair with that card to provide evidence for this topic. The rest of the class should listen to the evidence and try to argue. Continue the mini-debates until most or all students have had a chance to defend the topic they were assigned.

5. After this exercise, ask students to write in their journals and note the three pieces of evidence that they found most compelling in the discussions. They may use this in their papers later on.

REPRODUCIBLE 14.1 Sample Card Topics for Prompt #1

Governor Orval Faubus	Parents of the Little Rock Nine	Brown v. Board of Ed.
The Constitution	T.V.	Daisy Bates
NAACP	Thurgood Marshall	Superintendent Virgil Blossom
101st Airborne Division	White student allies	Grace Lorch

Directions: Answer the following questions about the subject of your card.

_____ should be honored or commemorated because	
Reason #1	Evidence to support this argument:
Reason #2	Evidence to support this argument:
Reason #3	Evidence to support this argument:

Can you think of one reason why _____ should not be honored for their contributions to the desegregation of Central High School?

Reason	Evidence to support this argument:

STRATEGY 15. Linking Claims and Evidence with Analysis

WRITING FOCUS: Analyze evidence.

COMMON CORE ALIGNMENT: Work with peers to set rules for collegial discussions and decision-making (e.g., informal consensus, taking votes on key issues, presentation of alternate views), clear goals and deadlines, and individual roles as needed. (WHST.9-10.1b)

RATIONALE

Analysis/explanation is the link or the "glue" that holds the evidence and claim together,*[3] *explaining how and why the evidence helps prove the claim. The ability to analyze evidence is central to the study of history; students need to read data or source documents and be able to form interpretations or conclusions. Students benefit from opportunities to analyze and explain evidence orally, as "thinking," before trying to put that thinking into more formal written form in the body paragraphs of their essays. Students need to learn how to craft "warrants,"[4] a basic explanation of how their evidence proves their claim. One good way for them to learn this is to give them various pieces of evidence and various claims and have them practice connecting the two.

PROCEDURE

This strategy is best used immediately after the Building Arguments strategy.

1. After completing the card activity, ask students to link the claims with the evidence. Which evidence proves which claims? Use a three-column chart to record answers. (See **Reproducible 15.1**.)

   - *Left: Claims.* Teacher completes in advance, listing claims students need to prove.

   - *Middle: Evidence.* Students complete first. They either paste in evidence that has been cut up into strips or write in evidence they gather themselves.

   - *Right: Analysis.* Students complete last. This is where they explain *how* the evidence in the middle connects or proves the claim on the left.

2. Ask them to justify their choices, using the following prompts:

   - What does this piece of evidence prove? What makes you say that?

   - How does this piece of evidence prove X? Explain your thinking.

   - What else might this evidence prove?

   - Why is this evidence important?

   - What does this evidence show?

---

[3] Andrea A. Lunsford and John J. Ruszkiewicz, *Everything's an Argument*, 2nd ed. (New York: Bedford/St. Martin's, 2001), 95.

[4] Stephen Toulmin, *The Uses of Argument* (Cambridge, UK: Cambridge University Press, 1958).

REPRODUCIBLE 15.1 Three-Column Chart Linking Claims, Evidence, and Analysis

CLAIM	EVIDENCE	ANALYSIS ← → (How does the evidence prove the claim?)
(Teacher provides the claim.) Individuals are powerful and can change society.	*(Student first finds evidence to support the claim.)* A group of students in college decided to go on the Freedom Rides. Because of the Freedom Rides, the president of the United States eventually got involved and states were forced to obey the laws that said transportation could no longer be segregated.	*(Student then links the evidence with the claim.)* This shows that even ordinary college students were able to change the behavior of government officials—both the President and the leaders of several Southern states.

STRATEGY 16. Thesis Sorting

WRITING FOCUS: Students will identify several possible thesis statements that address the same essay prompt and evaluate the strengths and weaknesses of each.

COMMON CORE ALIGNMENT: Write arguments focused on discipline-specific content; introduce claim(s) about a topic or issue, distinguish the claim(s) from alternate or opposing claims, and create an organization that establishes clear relationships among the claim(s), counterclaims, reasons and evidence. (WHST.9-19.1a)

RATIONALE

This strategy promotes critical thinking, since in crafting a thesis students are required to put their own ideas in conversation with the text. Sometimes a prompt directs students to one obvious thesis statement when there are actually other more nuanced arguments they could make. The purpose of this activity is to help generate the possible arguments that could be made based on the same prompt and for students to understand the elements of a successful thesis.

PROCEDURE

1. **Make Sure Students Understand the Prompt.** See the Dissecting the Prompt strategy on page 22.

2. **Brainstorm Options.** This could be done as a small group or a whole-class activity. Before having students do a thesis brainstorm for the first time, you might want to model it using a different prompt.

    Example

    Prompt: Margaret Mead, an anthropologist (a scientist who studies people and culture) said, "Never doubt that a small group of thoughtful, committed citizens can change the world. Indeed, it is the only thing that ever has." You have just learned about events during the civil rights movement. Writean essay in which you explain how this history supports or refutes Margaret Mead's statement.

    Some thesis options:

    Option 1: The history of the civil rights movement supports Margaret Mead's statement because . . .

    Option 2: The history of the civil rights movement refutes Margaret Mead's statement because . . .

    Option 3: While thoughtful groups of committed citizens contributed to the civil rights movement, _____, _____, and (optional) _____ also played significant roles in this history.

3. **Students Practice Writing Excellent, Good, and Weak Thesis Statements.** After you feel that students understand how to write a thesis, put them into groups of two or three. Ask them to write three thesis statements on different

slips of paper. One thesis should be excellent, one good, and one intentionally weak. Before this step, you might want to review the criteria for a good thesis. In general, a good thesis:

- takes a clear stance on an issue,
- addresses *all* elements of the prompt, and
- can be defended with evidence.

An especially strong thesis presents an especially original argument and/or articulates a nuanced or more refined argument.

4. **Students Categorize and Sort Thesis Statements.** After each group has practiced writing different thesis statements, pass out a list of thesis statements that you have already written. We recommend cutting these up so that each statement is on a separate strip of paper. Make sure your list includes excellent, good, and weak theses. You can also include some of the statements that students just wrote in their groups.

   In the same groups, ask students to try to categorize the thesis statements into the categories of excellent, good, and weak. Make sure they are using some of the above criteria to make their decisions.

   After the groups are finished, ask students to walk around the room and visit other groups' categories. Tell students to notice how different groups interpreted or categorized the same thesis statements.

5. **Debrief and Assessment.** When students return to their original lists, have a class discussion about what they noticed. Where in the class does there seem to be disagreement? confusion? consistency? What is the difference between an excellent, good, and weak thesis statement?

   During the discussion, make sure you correct any clear misunderstandings about thesis statements.

   As an informal assessment, ask groups to pick two thesis statements in the weak and good categories. Tell the group to edit each thesis statement so that they feel it can move up one category (from weak to good or from good to excellent).

STRATEGY 17. Tug for Truth

This strategy is adapted from and used with the permission of Project Zero.[5]

WRITING FOCUS: Students practice evidence-based reasoning skills.

COMMON CORE ALIGNMENT: Write arguments focused on discipline-specific content; introduce precise claims and distinguish the claim from alternate or opposing claims (WHST.9-10.1a)

RATIONALE

This strategy encourages students to reason carefully about the "pull" of various factors that are relevant to a question of truth. It also helps them appreciate the deeper complexity of matters of truth that can appear black and white on the surface.

PROCEDURE

This strategy builds on students' familiarity with the game of tug-of-war to help them understand the complex forces that "tug" at either side of a question of truth. The strategy uses a rope or a diagram to represent pulls toward true or false in evaluating a claim. The tug-of-war is between true and false. Help students think about the various factors that tug at one side of the rope or the other, as well as other considerations related to the issue.

1. Identify a question of truth—a controversial claim that something is true or false—where you know there is some evidence on both sides that students can bring forward.

2. Ask students if they have an opinion about it.

3. Draw a tug-of-war diagram on the board (or tape a piece of rope on the wall and use self-stick notes to make it more dramatic). Explain that students can add two kinds of things. One is evidence—tugs in the yes or true direction or in the no or false direction. The other thing to add is a question about the tug-of-war itself, a question that asks for more information or about "what if"—if we tried this or we tried that, what would the results be?

4. Finish the lesson by asking students what new ideas they have about the question of truth:

    - Can we decide now?

    - Do some people lean one way and some the other?

    - Is the best answer in a "gray area"—most of the time true but not always, or true half the time?

---

[5] "Introduction to Thinking Routines," accessed October 22, 2011, http://www.visiblethinkingpz.org/VisibleThinking_html_files/VisibleThinking1.html.

STRATEGY 18. Refuting Counterarguments

WRITING FOCUS: Students learn to write and challenge counterarguments.

COMMON CORE ALIGNMENT: Introduce precise claim(s), distinguish the claim(s) from alternate or opposing claims, and create an organization that establishes clear relationships among the claim(s), counterclaims, reasons, and evidence. (WHST.9-10.1a)

RATIONALE

In order to write a strong argumentative paper, students need to both anticipate and refute counterarguments to their thesis. This strategy asks students to focus specifically on counterclaims that others may have when reading their ideas. It also promotes critical thinking, since considering and refuting counterarguments requires students to consider an issue from multiple points of view.

PROCEDURE

1. In the tenth grade, students are required to include a counterargument in their essay. Using an argument the class has brainstormed, show students how someone might respond with a counterargument.

2. Then have the class help you refute this counterargument, drawing on historical evidence. You might want to do this twice before asking students to refute counterarguments on their own.

3. Students can use **Reproducible 18.1** to practice working with counterarguments. They can complete worksheets with a partner.

4. Students begin with their own worksheet by completing row 1.

5. Then, they switch with their partner and complete row 2.

6. Next, they switch back and complete row 3.

7. Finally, they end with their partner's paper when completing row 4.

8. At the end of this exercise, students can discuss which of the arguments on the page is the strongest and why. This strategy can also be used to help students prepare for a SPAR debate (see Strategy 13).

REPRODUCIBLE 18.1 Sample Counterargument Worksheet

WORD BANK				
	Useful language to use when making and refuting counterarguments				
Nevertheless	Some might believe	But	Even so	Despite
On the one hand	On the other hand	While	It is true	Yet
In contrast	To some extent	Although	Admittedly	However
It might seem that	What this argument fails to account for			

1. Argument This thesis is true because . . .	
2. Counterargument Yet some people argue . . .	
3. Refutation But . . .	
4. Response On the other hand . . .	

facinghistory.org

D. PROVING YOUR POINT THROUGH LOGICAL REASONING IN BODY PARAGRAPHS

Use these strategies **after** *the unit.*

Once students have identified and organized their thesis, arguments, and evidence, they are ready to begin crafting these ideas into coherent paragraphs.

Argumentative essays typically have one "central" argument (the thesis or central claim) and multiple smaller arguments in which the author presents a claim or reason, cites evidence, and offers analysis. This analysis, technically called a "warrant," is the glue holding claims and evidence together. In this section, we include strategies to help students practice linking claims, evidence, and analysis orally. We also include ways to help students learn more flexible ways to present those ideas so their writing feels fresh, not formulaic.

Many teachers offer students a mini-lesson on an aspect of writing, such as outlining or using transitions, and then give them class time to apply these lessons to their own writing. One of the challenges in supporting students-as-writers is in giving them enough freedom to find their own voice and providing sufficient structure to help them craft a thoughtful, thorough, well-organized essay. Some students will benefit from having clear guidelines, such as graphic organizers to complete, especially if this is their first experience writing a formal, argumentative essay. Students who already understand the basic components of an essay may not need these supports.

STRATEGY 19. Claims, Data, and Analysis

WRITING FOCUS: Analyze evidence in writing.

COMMON CORE ALIGNMENT: Develop claim(s) and counterclaims fairly, supplying data and evidence for each while pointing out the strengths and limitations of both claim(s) and counterclaims in a discipline-appropriate form and in a manner that anticipates the audience's knowledge level and concerns. (WHST.9-10.1b)

RATIONALE

Strong body paragraphs include claims, evidence or "data," and analysis or "warrants."[6] Writers can visualize these three components as a balancing scale. The three components can be put in any order; students need not perceive this as a "formula" to follow.

The ability to analyze evidence is central to the study of history; students need to read data or source documents and be able to form interpretations or conclusions. Once students have had many chances to practice analyzing and explaining evidence orally, they can begin to put their thinking into a more formal written structure: the body paragraphs of their argumentative essay.

We want students to move away from formulaic body paragraphs (in which they always introduce a claim first, then cite evidence, and then explain how the evidence proves the claim). Once students understand Toulmin's model for argument—in which one states a claim, provides evidence, and then explains *how* the evidence proves the claim—they can start to mix and match these three elements more flexibly.

PROCEDURE

1. Show students an example of a strong analytical paragraph. (This could be a paragraph from a former student or from **Reproducible 19.1**).

2. Discuss the ideas in the paragraph. What is the author claiming? Proving? Then discuss how the author crafts his or her argument.

3. On chart paper or on your computer projected to a Smartboard, draw the balancing scale. Label the two scales "claim" and "evidence." Label the fulcrum "analysis/warrant." Put this chart somewhere that allows you to refer back to it in the coming weeks.

---

6 Stephen Toulmin, *The Uses of Argument* (Cambridge, UK: Cambridge University Press, 1958).

4. On a big strip of paper, or on your computer projected to a Smartboard, write a simple real-world claim for which you can cite evidence. (Perhaps use a claim that says something positive about the students as a group—e.g., "This class is very responsible"—or about some current event/issue at school. You could also use an example from your current Facing History unit or a previous unit they all will remember.)

5. Next, ask students to cite evidence to prove the claim (e.g., "We come to class prepared," "We ask questions when we need help"). Write the evidence on a separate big strip of paper or in a different color on your computer.

6. Then, ask them to provide warrants to link the evidence to the claim (e.g., "Students who are responsible know that it is their job to understand the material and aren't shy about asking for help if they are confused. That's how you get smarter"). Again, write this on a third big strip of paper or in a third type color on your computer.

7. Physically manipulate the three strips, or cut and paste on the computer, to show students the various ways these three sentences could be linked. After you show each variation, ask students to talk with a partner about whether they think this variation makes sense, is effective, etc. After all three, ask students to talk about which was best and why. They should be able to determine that there is in fact no "best"—just different ways of including these various components of an argument.

8. Ask students to do the same thing for a claim for their essay and have a partner critique it.

EXTENSION

After trying out different kinds of analysis, try writing your sentence strips in different orders. What do you gain or lose from each structure?

1, 2, 3 (claim, evidence, analysis)

2, 1, 3 (evidence, claim, analysis)

3, 1, 2 (analysis, claim, evidence)

(*See* **Reproducible 19.1**.)

REPRODUCIBLE 19.1 Claims, Evidence, and Analysis

Here are different ideas for how you can link claims and evidence with analysis.

- Make an inference. (*It seems that because of _____, _____ happened.*)

- Give an opinion. (*The decision to do _____ was dangerous because . . .*)

- Give a reason. (*He made this choice because . . .*)

- Give an effect. (*Because of this decision . . .*)

- Explain the importance. (*This is significant because . . .*)

- Compare and contrast with something. (*This is different from _____ because . . .*)

- Make an "if, then" statement. (*If this happened, then . . .*)

- Make a connection to another event or to ideas, past or present. (*This is similar to . . .*)

STRATEGY 20. Using Exemplars (or Mentor Texts)

WRITING FOCUS: Students will be able to identify the different parts of successful formal argumentative writing.

COMMON CORE ALIGNMENT: Produce clear and coherent writing in which the development, organization, and style are appropriate to task, purpose, and audience. (WHST.9-10.4)

RATIONALE

Using models or mentor texts engages students actively in inquiry, helping them to envision what strong writing looks and sounds like and to construct criteria for their own writing.

PROCEDURE

1. **Locate Exemplars.** Both student and "expert" (professional) writing can be used as exemplars. Students can read entire essays or only one paragraph. Exemplars you might use include writing by your students; your own writing; professional writing, such as newspaper editorials; and the student writing from this resource, found in **Reproducibles 21.1**, **24.1**, and **27.1**.

2. **Active Reading of Exemplars.** Often it is easier to recognize qualities of effective (and ineffective) writing when texts are read aloud. Ask a volunteer to read the exemplar aloud while the rest of the class marks up the text. Students can underline main ideas and place question marks near sentences that are unclear. You might ask students to distinguish between evidence and analysis of this evidence.

3. **Evaluating Exemplars.** Whether students are reading one exemplar or several, it helps to give them a rubric they can use to evaluate the writing. Ideally, this is the same rubric that will be used to evaluate their writing. By participating in a discussion about the strengths and weaknesses of writing, students gain a deeper understanding of what they should aspire to produce in their own writing.

4. **Reflective Journal Writing.** Possible prompts for reflection include: What makes some writing better than other writing? What lessons from this exercise will you apply to your own writing?

VARIATION

Fill in the Essay: To help build particular writing skills, you could distribute incomplete exemplar essays to students and ask them to fill in the missing parts. For example, you could have students read several body paragraphs and then ask them to write an introduction or conclusion for that essay. Or you could give students an exemplar with only claims and evidence and ask them to add analysis.

STRATEGY 21. Looking at Student Work: Body Paragraphs

WRITING FOCUS: Students will read other student work to look at patterns of writing claims, evidence, and analysis in a body paragraph.

COMMON CORE ALIGNMENT: Write arguments focused on *discipline-specific content*. (WHST.9-10.1)

RATIONALE

Looking at other students' work can help students think about their own writing. In this activity, students will read other student samples to think about how claims, evidence, and analysis work together in a body paragraph. They will also practice revising student paragraphs to help prepare them for beginning their own writing.

PROCEDURE

1. Prepare students to read the student samples provided in **Reproducible 21.1**. Tell them that they will be reading real student samples and that their job is to highlight the claims, evidence, and analysis that they see in each paragraph.

2. To make it simpler, when students read, have them highlight claims in yellow, evidence in blue, and analysis in green. It may be easier to do this on computers if you have access to technology. If you do not have access to technology or access to colored highlighters or crayons, have students underline the claims, circle the evidence, and put a box around the analysis.

3. After students complete this for one paragraph, talk about what they found. Sample questions include:
   - What did you like about the paragraph? What did the writer do well?
   - Did the claims, evidence, and analysis always come in the same order?
   - What was missing? Did the writer have more evidence or analysis? How do you know?
   - What advice would you give to the writer if he or she were sitting next to you?

4. Next, ask students to revise the paragraph. They can do this individually, in groups, or as a whole class. If you have a Smartboard, you might project the paragraph and revise the first one together using track changes.

5. After going through at least one paragraph together, have students analyze the remaining body paragraphs.

REPRODUCIBLE 21.1 Sample Body Paragraphs from Students

An example of an individual having power is Mamie Till Mobley. Two white men had brutally murdered her son, Emmett Till. She made efforts for the nation to see what had happened to her son in the South. She, broadcasting those images, influenced many to join the Civil Rights Movement and also got the attention of the nation. Some may argue that she did not have the power, that it was all the media. Without the media, she would have never been known by the nation, and zero attention would be drawn to the South. Also, not a lot of people would have joined the movement otherwise. Despite what they may argue, she is an individual had the power. The media was merely a tool for her to use to get the news out around the nation. Without her story, the media wouldn't have a story.

Bob Moses shows that an individual can change a society by using organizations. Moses joined a group called SNCC (Student Nonviolent Coordinating Committee) in 1960 through SNCC Moses was able to arrange Freedom Summer, a program in which volunteers, regardless of race from all over the country would came and educated Black Americans about voting and to get them to register to vote. The reason they wanted them to vote was to for them to have a voice about their communities so a change can be made. Some may say that even though the Freedom Summers helped, Moses would not have been successful if it weren't for the volunteers who had participated in the program in the first place. Others, argue that without Moses being there the Freedom Summer would not have existed and volunteers wouldn't have come in the first place because people would not be motivated to do so.

John Hardy was young Black college student who wanted to educate other Black Americans about their voting rights and how they can affect their community. Hardy went to Mississippi to help give Blacks the knowledge and courage to register to vote in a state where a Black man's decision to do so could cost him his home, his job and/or his life. While in Mississippi he escorted a 63-year-old woman and a 62-year-old man he had worked with to the county registrar's office. The registrar refused to register them. He cursed Hardy and ordered him out of his office. As Hardy was leaving, the registrar grabbed a pistol and struck Hardy so hard that he stumbled. He was thrown in jail for disturbing the peace, when he came out he was more determined than ever to get Black Americans to register. Hardy served on the Freedom Ride Coordinating Committee of SNCC, the Student Nonviolent Coordinating Committee. After a while the Mississippi authorities ran him out of town, Hardy and Black Mississippians eventually were victorious. This made other Black individuals want to follow Hardy in his cause to get voting rights to African Americans. A U.S. Court of Appeals decision agreed that the continued prosecution of Hardy "was designed to and would intimidate qualified Negroes of Walthall County from attempting to register to vote." The federal court also affirmed the rights of qualified Black citizens in Mississippi to vote. People say that if it weren't for the Black citizens who wanted to vote, Hardy would have accomplished nothing, however if he did not appeal to Black citizens they would not have accomplished any thing.

The Freedom Riders were a mixed group of Black and white individuals who stood up to change society. In order to help out Black Americans in their struggle for equality, the Freedom Riders were people who made an effort to test a Supreme Court ruling. This was done by them boarding buses that were intended for one ethnic group. Some might believe that the Freedom Riders group wouldn't really count as an individual, and what they did caused more harm than it did any good. However, the Freedom Riders were all individuals. They acted on their own free will, and in the end, fought to achieve their goal.

STRATEGY 22. Using Graphic Organizers to Organize Writing

WRITING FOCUS: Students will organize main ideas, evidence, and analysis before they begin writing.

COMMON CORE ALIGNMENT: Introduce precise claim(s), distinguish the claim(s) from alternate or opposing claims, and create an organization that establishes clear relationships among the claim(s), counterclaims, reasons, and evidence. (WHST.9-10.1a)

Develop claim(s) and counterclaims fairly, supplying data and evidence for each while pointing out the strengths and limitations of both claim(s) and counterclaims in a discipline-appropriate form and in a manner that anticipates the audience's knowledge level and concerns. (WHST.9-10.1b)

RATIONALE

Graphic organizers can help students put their ideas in a logical order and notice where they need more information. You might have all students complete a graphic organizer before writing (or typing) their essays, or you might make this an option for students. By breaking a whole paper into smaller, clear tasks, graphic organizers are especially helpful for students who are unfamiliar with formal essay writing or who struggle with organizing ideas in writing.

One of the challenges in supporting students-as-writers is in giving them enough freedom to find their own voice and providing sufficient structure to help them craft a thoughtful, thorough, well-organized essay. We know that most educators teach students of varying abilities and therefore need several different avenues into an assignment. The graphic organizers that follow are suggestions to use with some of your students who may need extra scaffolds to outline a writing assignment. Some students will benefit from having clear structures, such as graphic organizers to complete, especially if this is their first experience writing a formal, argumentative essay. Students who already understand the basic components of an essay may not need these supports.

PROCEDURE

1. **Select a Graphic Organizer to Use.** There are many ways to visually organize an essay. Some samples are included here as Reproducibles, or you can also find other examples online, such as the Sandwich Graphic Organizer and the Persuasion Plan. A graphic organizer provided in this packet uses the MEAL structure to help students organize their ideas:

    - **M**ain idea (argument)
    - **E**vidence that supports that main idea
    - **A**nalysis to explain how the evidence proves the main idea
    - **L**ink between the argument and the thesis statement

2. **Model How to Complete It.** You might show students what an organizer looks like that is complete, or you can complete an organizer together with students. Most teachers only require students to write words and phrases on their graphic organizers, not complete sentences. Whatever you decide, be sure to communicate this to students.

3. **Students Complete the Graphic Organizer in Class and/or at Home.** Often it can help students to have a partner review their work and help them when they get stuck.

4. **Review Graphic Organizers before Students Begin Writing or Typing Their Essays.** Often teachers sign off on students' outline or graphic organizer before students proceed to the writing phase. If students begin the writing with clearly organized ideas, they are less likely to be frustrated with the task of crafting coherent sentences.

REPRODUCIBLE 22.1 Sample Concept Map Graphic Organizer

Directions: Fill in the circles with your thesis and arguments. Connect relevant evidence to each argument.

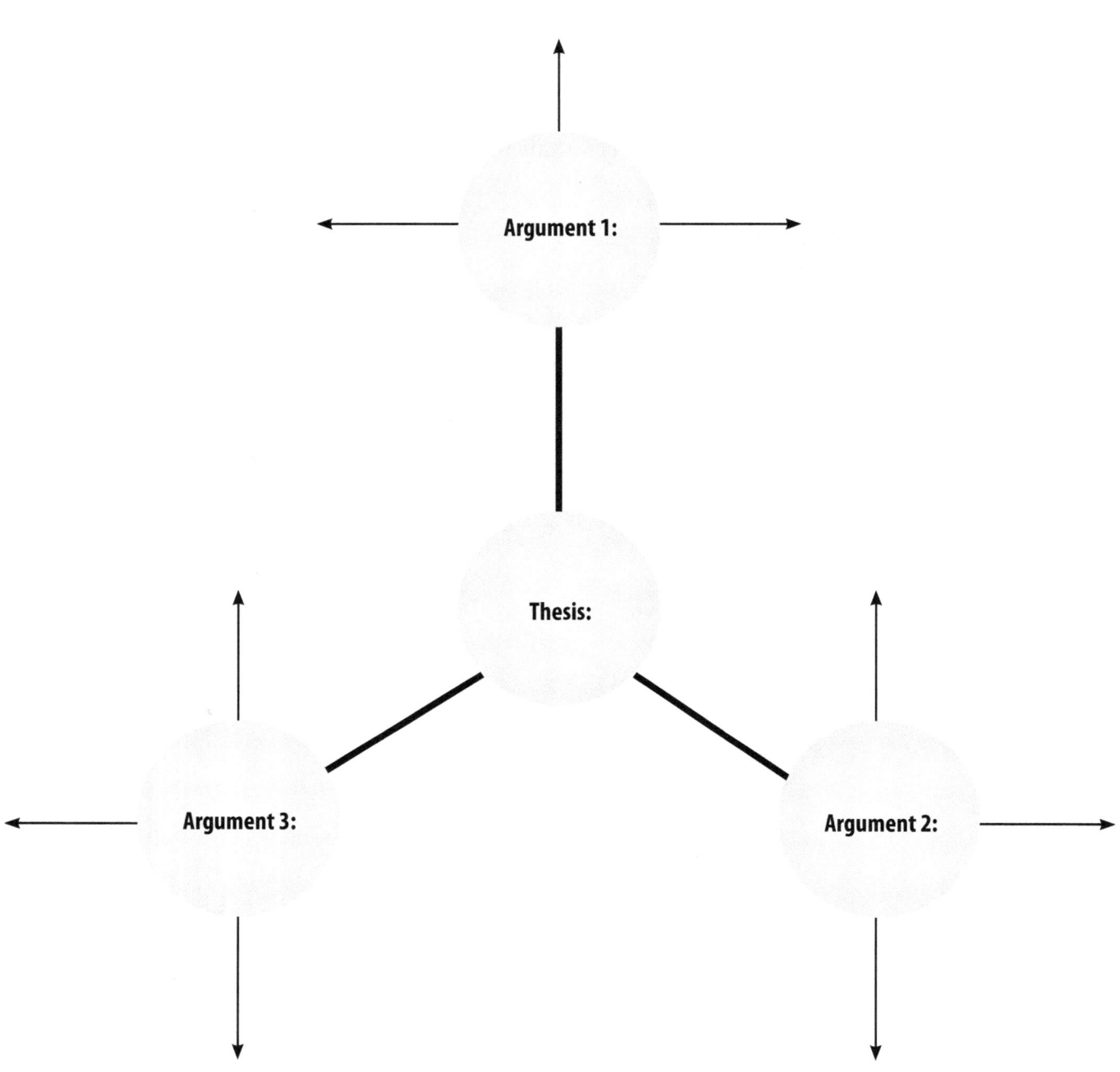

REPRODUCIBLE 22.2 Outlining Your Essay: Graphic Organizer for Body Paragraph (with feedback sheet)

OUTLINE FOR BODY PARAGRAPH # _____

THESIS (The purpose of my paper is to prove . . .):

ARGUMENT (This thesis is true because . . .):

Evidence to support argument (with citation):	**Analysis:** *This evidence supports my argument because . . .*
1.	
2.	
3.	

(Optional)

COUNTERARGUMENT *(Some people argue . . .)*:

Evidence to refute counterargument (with citation):	**Analysis:** *This evidence refutes the counterargument because . . .*

Feedback on Body Paragraph Outline

Author's name:

Editor's name:

This is for feedback on body paragraph # _____

Clarity of argument: _____ points

_____ Argument supports thesis statement. (1 point)

_____ Argument does not support thesis statement. (0 points)

Strength of evidence: _____ points

_____ Includes two or more pieces of relevant, high-quality evidence. (3 points)

_____ Includes one piece of relevant, high-quality evidence. (2 points)

_____ Evidence provided but does not support argument or is not high-quality—not from sources we have used in class or other approved source. (1 point)

_____ Relevant counterargument is refuted with evidence. (1 point)

_____ No evidence provided. (no points)

Citing sources: _____ points

_____ Cites all sources appropriately. (2 points)

_____ Cites sources but does not always follow proper format. (1 point)

_____ No citations. (no points)

Analysis: _____ points

_____ Clearly explains how evidence supports argument. (2 points)

_____ Explains how some, but not all, evidence supports argument. (1 point)

_____ Does not explain how evidence supports argument. (0 points)

Suggested next steps:

STRATEGY 23. Sentence-Strip Paragraphs

WRITING FOCUS: Students will learn to organize their thinking into paragraphs.

COMMON CORE ALIGNMENT: Introduce precise claim(s), distinguish the claim(s) from alternate or opposing claims, and create an organization that establishes clear relationships among the claim(s), counterclaims, reasons, and evidence. (WHST.9-10.1a)

Develop claim(s) and counterclaims fairly, supplying data and evidence for each while pointing out the strengths and limitations of both claim(s) and counterclaims in a discipline-appropriate form and in a manner that anticipates the audience's knowledge level and concerns. (WHST.9-10.1b)

RATIONALE

This strategy can be used to help students organize introductory, body, and concluding paragraphs. It has students moving around sentences on slips of paper to help them learn how to organize their ideas in a paragraph. It also should remind students of the earlier analysis activities that they used when crafting their thesis and organizing their ideas.

PROCEDURE

1. **Preparation.** Divide students into groups of four or five. Cut strips of paper and give each group at least ten. This activity could also be done with students working individually or in pairs.

2. **Write Sentences on Strips of Paper.** Students write one sentence on each strip. The type of paragraph you focus on for this activity will determine what you ask groups to write on their slips. For example, if you are using this activity to help students write introductory paragraphs, you would want one group to record possible hooks for the essay, another group to record sentences that would go in the background section, and another group to record possible thesis statements. If you are using this activity to help students write body paragraphs, you might assign a group a particular argument and have them record possible evidence on separate strips of paper.

3. **Share Strips.** Students can either tape their strips to a large piece of paper or leave them on their table.

4. **Build a Paragraph.** Individually or in groups, have students go around the room looking for ideas to help build their paragraphs. Sometimes teachers have students tape the selected strips in order to create a paragraph. Students can also record the sentences or ideas they want to use on a graphic organizer, such as their Inverted Pyramid (see Strategy 24).

5. **Fill in Gaps.** After students build a paragraph with sentence strips, ask them to fill in gaps with new sentences. Gaps might include transition words linking one idea to the next or analysis that explains how evidence connects to the

main idea of the paragraph. Sentence starters you might use to help students add analysis statements include:

- *This evidence shows that . . .*
- *Therefore . . .*
- *These examples demonstrate . . .*
- *Because _____, then _____.*
- *Clearly, this suggests that . . .*
- *This evidence is an example of . . .*
- *This reveals that . . .*

VARIATION

Using Exemplars: To help students practice organizing ideas, you can cut an exemplar essay, such as the one included in the Using Exemplars teaching strategy (Strategy 20), into sentence strips and then have students place these sentences in an order that makes sense.

E. FRAMING AND CONNECTING IDEAS IN INTRODUCTIONS AND CONCLUSIONS

Use these strategies **after** *the unit.*

As students develop their argument, it is also important that they keep the "So what?" question in mind. A central mission of Facing History is to help students make connections between history and the choices they make in their own lives. We want them not only to engage with the evidence logically but also to engage emotionally and ethically, considering implications for the present and the future.

When writing a formal essay, students demonstrate that they can make these big conceptual connections mostly in the opening and closing paragraphs. In this section, we include strategies that support students in first *making* those connections to the here and now and then expressing those connections in ways that are clear and compelling to their audience.

STRATEGY 24. Introductions: Inverted Pyramid

WRITING FOCUS: Students will write an organized introductory paragraph, including a hook, background information, and thesis.

COMMON CORE ALIGNMENT: Introduce precise claim(s) about a topic or issue, distinguish the claim(s) from alternate or opposing claims, and create an organization that establishes clear relationships among the claim(s), counterclaims, reasons and evidence. (WHST.9-10.1a)

RATIONALE

The Inverted Pyramid is a structure that represents how an introductory paragraph is typically organized. This strategy helps students understand the content that needs to be included in an introduction and visualize where it should be placed. This activity might be most appropriate when students are ready to write their papers, after they have selected their thesis and homed in on their arguments.

PROCEDURE

1. **Preparation.** For this activity students can use a graphic organizer, or they can draw their own upside-down pyramids in their notebooks. The pyramid should be divided into three sections.

2. **Ask Students to Label the Pyramid.** Tell them that this pyramid represents the introduction to their paper. Give them the following terms and definitions and ask them to label where on the pyramid they think it makes sense to place this information. You could also ask students to label these parts on a persuasive essay you give to them as an exemplar.

    - *Hook:* A hook is a sentence or question that captures the reader's attention—by addressing something that connects to their lives or providing particularly interesting or surprising information. It can also be a general statement that sets the tone for the essay.

    - *Background Information:* To understand an essay, readers often need some background information on a topic. For example, your reader may never have heard about Central High School or Little Rock, Arkansas, or Jim Crow segregation. Writers often use the introduction to provide readers with the basic facts needed to understand the essay.

    - *Thesis Statement:* The *point* of an argumentative essay is to persuade the reader to believe a claim you are making. The main claim of your essay is called the thesis statement.

3. **Have Students Review Other Sample Introductions (see Reproducible 24.1).** As students read the examples, ask them to label the hook, the background information, and the thesis statement. Ask them questions about the sample paragraphs: What do you like about the introduction? Is anything missing? How might you enhance or rework this introduction?

REPRODUCIBLE 24.1 Introductory Paragraphs from Students

The Civil Right Movement was a hopeful period of time in American history that was full of individuals who were willing to stand up and take a risk for what they believed in with the help and support from others. Public segregation and discrimination happened mostly in the South. The Movement lasted for more than 3 years, which is a very long time and a lot of people had sacrificed their lives. Injustice things that happened were countless, The evidence shows that an individual could change society through risky actions, words, and courage. Just like the people that stood up for their rights back then, there's many more that do that today. If there was anything I would like anyone to get out of the history of the Civil Rights Movement it would be everything that happened before hand to make this movement possible. The tragedies that happened to many people that were either black or white were wrong no matter what logical reasoning there could of possibly been, racial violence was definitely not the answer. It all leads back to the question if an individual has power. If no one had a voice to speak up, then there would still be no change, so whether it was having power as a group or an individual, everyone still had their own power as one because their words mattered when they spoke. Every person as one had a voice, they had power and they made this change possible.

African Americans did not have the right to vote and children were not able to get a proper education which they deserved. A lot of individuals decided to stand up and take action to change the society, such as Mamie-Till Mobley and Mose Wright. Although, they couldn't have been able to do what they did without help from others. During the Civil Rights Movement, an individual did not have enough power to change the society on their own; there were major help from the media, supports from other individuals and mainly, the decisions of the government.

STRATEGY 25. Conclusions: Text-to-Text, Text-to-Self, Text-to-World

WRITING FOCUS: Students will identify connections between the ideas in their essays and their own lives and gather ideas they might use in their concluding paragraph.

COMMON CORE ALIGNMENT: Provide a concluding statement or section that follows from or supports the argument presented. (WHST.9-10.1e)

RATIONALE

In the conclusion of an essay, students help the reader understand how the ideas in the essay connect to other events in the past and present. This helps the reader appreciate why the ideas in the essay matter. Text-to-Text, Text-to-Self, Text-to-World is a strategy that helps students develop the habit of making these connections. It can be used to help students prepare for writing a conclusion, after they have written the body paragraphs of their essay.

PROCEDURE

1. **Preparation.** Students need a copy of their essay for this activity. You might also want to prepare a graphic organizer for them to do this activity. Or they could answer the questions in a notebook or journal.

2. **Active Reading with Text-to-Text, Text-to-Self, Text-to-World.** Below are sample directions and prompts you can use with this strategy:

    - *Text-to-Text*—How do the ideas in your essay remind you of another text (story, book, movie, song, document, etc.)?
    - *Text-to-Self*—How do the ideas in your essay relate to your own life, ideas, and experiences?
    - *Text-to-World*—How do the ideas in your essay relate to the larger world—past, present, and future?

3. **Debrief and Journal Writing.** Students gain a deeper understanding of their essays, their classmates, and the world around them when they have the opportunity to discuss their responses with peers. Students can share their responses with a partner, in small groups, or as part of a larger discussion.

    Possible journal prompts include:

    - What ideas are on your mind now about how to conclude your paper?
    - Of all the ideas you recorded, which one is the most interesting to you? Why?

STRATEGY 26. Fishbowl

WRITING FOCUS: Students will discuss the relevance of the ideas in their essay and practice thinking they will use in their concluding paragraph.

COMMON CORE ALIGNMENT: Provide a concluding statement or section that follows from or supports the argument presented. (WHST.9-10.1e)

RATIONALE

As thinkers and writers, students need practice contributing to and listening to a discussion. The Fishbowl is a teaching strategy that helps students practice being contributors and listeners in a discussion. Students ask questions, present opinions, and share information when they sit in the Fishbowl circle while students on the outside of the circle listen carefully to the ideas presented and pay attention to the process. Then the roles reverse. This strategy is especially useful when you want to make sure all students participate in the discussion, help students reflect on what a good discussion looks like, and provide a structure for discussing controversial or difficult topics.

PROCEDURE

1. **Preparing Students for the Fishbowl.** For the purpose of helping students write conclusions for their essays, you might have students write about one of the following questions in their journals before beginning the Fishbowl discussion:

    - How do the ideas in your paper connect to life today? What is the same? What may be different?
    - What would you like someone to learn from reading your essay?
    - What did you learn from the *Civil Rights Historical Investigations* unit?
    - What questions are on your mind after writing this essay?

    The Text-to-Text, Text-to-Self, Text-to-World strategy also can be used to prepare students to participate in a Fishbowl discussion about the relevance of their essays.

2. **Setting Up the Room.** A Fishbowl requires a circle of chairs (the "fishbowl") and enough room around the circle for the remaining students to observe what is happening in the "fishbowl." Sometimes teachers place enough chairs for half of the students in the class to sit in the "fishbowl," while other times teachers limit the chairs in the "fishbowl." Typically having six to twelve chairs allows for a range of perspectives while still giving each student an opportunity to speak. The observing students often stand around the "fishbowl."

3. **Discussing Norms and Rules of the Discussion.** There are many ways to structure a Fishbowl discussion. Sometimes half the class will sit in the "fishbowl" for 10–15 minutes, and then the teacher will say, "Switch." At

this point the listeners enter the "fishbowl," and the speakers become the audience. Another common Fishbowl format is the "tap" system. When students on the outside of the "fishbowl" wish to join the discussion, they gently tap a student on the inside, and the two students switch roles.

Regardless of the particular rules you establish, you want to make sure these are explained to students beforehand. You also want to provide instructions for the students in the audience. What should they be listening for? Should they be taking notes? Before beginning the Fishbowl, you may wish to review guidelines for having a respectful conversation. Sometimes teachers ask audience members to pay attention to how these norms are followed by recording specific aspects of the discussion process, such as the number of interruptions, respectful or disrespectful language used, or speaking times (Who is speaking the most? The least?).

4. **Debriefing the Fishbowl Discussion and Journal Writing.** After the discussion, you can ask students to reflect on the ideas they heard that might be relevant for the conclusions of their essays. What ideas and questions interested them the most?

STRATEGY 27. Writing Conclusions after Looking at Student Samples

WRITING FOCUS: Students will evaluate other students' concluding paragraphs and gather ideas about how they might structure their own concluding paragraph.

COMMON CORE ALIGNMENT: Provide a concluding statement or section that follows from or supports the argument presented. (WHST.9-10.1e)

RATIONALE

In the conclusion of an essay, students help the reader understand how the ideas in the essay connect to other events in the past and present. Looking at models can be an effective way for students to gather ideas about how they might write their own conclusions.

PROCEDURE

1. Start with one or two of the student examples in **Reproducible 27.1**.
2. Ask students to respond to the following questions after reading the example:
   - What did the writer do well?
   - What did you learn from the writer?
   - Did the writer connect the ideas of his or her essay to other events in the past or present? (It might be helpful to have students underline where they see the writer making connections.)
   - If you were revising this conclusion, what would you do? What advice might you give the writer?
3. Ask students to pick one or two conclusions to revise. They can do this individually, in groups, or as a class. You could also project a paragraph onto a Smartboard and revise it together using track changes.
4. After revising a few paragraphs, ask students to practice writing their own concluding paragraphs for their essays.

REPRODUCIBLE 27.1 Conclusion Paragraphs from BPS Students

The preceding evidence demonstrates, that during the Civil Rights Movement, an individual had the power to change society. The examples of this would be Mamie Till Mobley, and how she made the efforts to bring in attention as to the violence, and injustice in the South. Mose Wright stood up against two white men, and became a symbol to the civil rights movement. Also how the Freedom Summer volunteers were able to help register people to vote and created freedom schools and community centers. This information is important because people need to know about the great sacrifices these individuals made to change our society today. Its important to see that there is hope. People should care because without these people standing up to make a difference, to make a powerful change to our society, we would not have what we do today. We would not have diverse schools and communities and Black people would not have the chances to vote or get an education for that matter. These are the things African Americans went through so that future generations would not have to suffer the same fate. By their actions, it inspires the young generations of today to step up as individuals and make a change in their on communities. It is with great honor, respect and gratefulness that we should pay to these individuals having the power to change society.

In conclusion, an individual does have to power to change society; it can be through direct action, peaceful protesting, and group power. Mamie Till-Mobley was able to prove that through direct action, ones word can get out. The Freedom Riders showed that through working together and determination, progression towards a goal could be reached. And finally, Martin Luther King Jr. proved that an individual could bring a large amount of people together to listen to what he had to say, and even follow him. It is important for people to know that an individual has the power to change society because they'll know that they don't have to sit around while an injustice is occurring, they can stand up and make a change themselves.

Today there are still many types of injustice and people willing to stand up and make a difference. For example in schools more than ever people are standing up to stop bullies. I want people to see that winning doesn't always involve a group and that a huge group and one person's effort make a group strong. Even after writing this paper I am still dwelling on whether a person really has the power to change society or not. The evidence shows that during the civil right's movement individuals had the power to change society because of their ability to lead others their strength as groups and their ability to take action. Martin Luther King Jr. was able to get the marchers a safe passage during the march because he was a good leader. John hardy took the initiative to help African Americans get registered because of that African Americans understood the importance of trying to get registered. The Boston Parents were able to get a law passed to bus their kids out to a better school because they came together.

The evidence shows that an individual could change society through risky actions, words, and courage. Just like the people that stood up for their rights back then, there's many more that do that today. If there was anything I would like anyone to get out of the history of the Civil Rights Movement it would be everything that happened before hand to make this movement possible. The tragedies that happened to many people that were either black or white were wrong no matter what logical reasoning there could of possibly been, racial violence was definitely not the answer. It all leads back to the question if an individual has power. If no one had a voice to speak up, then there would still be no change, so whether it was having power as a group or an individual, everyone still had their own power as one because their words mattered when they spoke. Every person as one had a voice, they had power and they made this change possible.

F. REVISING AND EDITING TO IMPACT YOUR AUDIENCE

*Use these strategies **after** the unit.*

Throughout the drafting of their essay, *and* after students have a complete rough draft, students need opportunities to rethink, revise, and refine their understanding. Students can substantially improve their logic and expression when they receive clear, specific, constructive feedback.[7] They also become better readers of their own writing when they analyze and critique others' writing—both "mentor texts" from the real world[8] and their peers' writing.

During the revising stage, students clarify, reorganize, and strengthen the content of their paper. They might add evidence or elaborate on their analysis. Revising often involves adding transitions to connect ideas and moving content from one paragraph to another.

This section provides two sorts of "revising" strategies: peer feedback and self-assessment. Getting feedback from peers and teachers can help students recognize where their ideas are unclear and what they need to do to make their essay stronger. Students can also evaluate their own essay using the CWA rubric.

Note: While Facing History sees the importance of copyediting one's writing to address grammar, spelling, or punctuation errors, in this resource we emphasize the broader challenges of helping students continue to reexamine the historical content and issues and to develop and express their thinking clearly. Teachers may want to help students understand the distinction between "revising" (which literally means "to look again"), or reworking one's ideas, and the much more specific task of copyediting to make one's writing clear and error-free.

After students are confident in the content and organization of their writing, they can move on to edit and spell-check their paper. During editing, teachers may want to provide mini-lessons on trouble spots for students (e.g., properly citing sources, using commas, etc.).

---

[7] Richard Beach and Tom Friedrich, "Response to Writing," in *Handbook of Writing Research,* ed. C. A. McArthur, S. Graham, and J. Fitzgerald (New York: The Guilford Press, 2006), 222–234.

[8] Katie Wood Ray, *Study Driven: A Framework for Planning Units of Study in the Writing Workshop* (Portsmouth, NH: Heinemann, 2006).

STRATEGY 28. 3-2-1

WRITING FOCUS: Students will read a peer's essay and provide specific feedback. They will also receive feedback on their own writing.

COMMON CORE ALIGNMENT: Develop and strengthen writing as needed by planning, revising, editing, rewriting, or trying a new approach, focusing on addressing what is most significant for a specific purpose and audience. (WHST.9-10.5)

RATIONALE

This activity provides a quick, structured way for students to give and receive feedback. The 3-2-1 prompt can be adjusted to suit the needs of particular students and specific assignments. Teachers have also found that using this strategy can help them streamline the feedback-giving process.

As students give each other feedback, again remind them that your focus is broader than this specific essay. You are teaching "the writer, not the writing."[9] Encourage peers to focus on each other's growth and persistence as writers.

PROCEDURE

1. **Answering 3-2-1 Prompt.** After students read a paper (either their own or a peer's paper), ask them to identify:

   - **Three** things the writer did well
   - **Two** next steps the writer could take to make the paper better
   - **One** question they have about the paper

   You can vary this prompt to suit specific aspects of the writing journey. For example, students could be asked to identify:

   - **One** thesis statement
   - **Two** arguments that support the thesis
   - **Three** pieces of evidence that support each argument

   or

   - **Three** transition words
   - **Two** sources cited properly
   - **One** source that still needs to be cited

   Students can record their responses on editing sheets, on the essay itself, or on exit tickets.

2. **Debriefing.** Use students' 3-2-1 responses to help evaluate where students may need more support for their writing. What are they able to locate in each other's papers? What questions keep popping up?

---

9 Lucy Calkins, *The Art of Teaching Writing* (Portsmouth, NH: Heinemann, 1994).

STRATEGY 29. Adding Transitions

WRITING FOCUS: Students will identify functions of transition words and phrases and add such words as needed to make their essays more clear and coherent.

COMMON CORE ALIGNMENT: Use words, phrases, and clauses to link the major sections of the text, create cohesion, and clarify the relationships between claim(s) and reasons, between reasons and evidence, and between claim(s) and counterclaims. (WHST.9-10.1c)

RATIONALE

Transitions help the reader connect one idea to the next and often distinguish a well-organized paper from a difficult-to-read paper. Many students need instruction on how and when to add transitions to their writing. It is often helpful to wait until the revision process to add transitions to a paper.

PROCEDURE

1. **Give Students a List of Transition Words.** Many websites post lists of transition words. Michigan State University offers one such list. Here is a shorter list of transition words and phrases you might use to get started:

   - **To express a similar idea:** also, furthermore, in addition, likewise, moreover, similarly
   - **To express something that is a result of something else:** accordingly, as a result, consequently, for this reason, therefore, thus
   - **To demonstrate a point:** for example, for instance, for one thing
   - **To compare and contrast:** on the one hand, on the other hand, on the contrary, rather, similarly, yet, but, however, still, nevertheless, in contrast
   - **To show when something happens in a sequence of events:** to begin with, in the first place, at the same time, next
   - **To summarize:** in conclusion, in summary, to summarize, finally

2. **Help Students Recognize the Value of Transition Words.** One way to do this is to have students read a paragraph or two from a textbook with the transition words removed. Then have them read the same text again, with the transition words inserted.

3. **Have Students Mark on Their Papers Where Transition Words Belong.** You might ask students to place a star at specific places where they expect to see transition words, such as at the beginning of each body paragraph and between sentences in the body paragraphs.

4. **Students Add Transitions to Their Papers.** Using a transition word list, ask students to add a minimum number of transition words to their paper (perhaps five to seven). They can work on this individually and then trade papers with a partner to check each other's work.

STRATEGY 30. Backwards Outline

WRITING FOCUS: Students will get feedback on their own writing, particularly the organization of their essay.

COMMON CORE ALIGNMENT: Produce clear and coherent writing in which the development, organization, and style are appropriate to task, purpose, and audience. (WHST.9-10.4)

RATIONALE

When students have to create an outline of a paper they are reading, it not only helps them pay attention to the structure of the writing (main idea, supporting evidence, etc.) but also provides important feedback to the writer.

PROCEDURE

1. **Have Students Find Partners or Assign Partners.** Alternatively, you can collect papers and pass them out randomly. Just be sure that no student ends up with his or her own paper.

2. **Creating Backwards Outlines.** Sample directions:

   - You will create an outline of the paper you are reading.
   - The outline must include the thesis, main arguments, and supporting details you find in the paper.
   - You do not have to write in complete sentences. Just capture the main words and phrases.

   It is often helpful to create a blank outline for students to fill in for this exercise. (See **Reproducible 30.1**.) You can provide a sample completed outline so that students understand that they do not have to rewrite the entire essay on the outline.

3. **Review Feedback and Add Comments.** You can collect the essays and the outlines as a way to evaluate the degree to which students can identify the different parts of a paper. Then you can add your own responses and return the paper, with the outline, to the writer.

4. **Students Revise Papers.** Based on what is missing on their outline, students should revise their paper. If this is the first time you are using this strategy, you might want to review how students will know what they need to do next. For example, if they notice a blank section of their outline, their first step can be to fill in that section.

REPRODUCIBLE 30.1 Blank Argumentative Essay Outline

(Adapt this outline to fit the assignment.)

INTRODUCTION

Hook:

Background information:

1) _____

2) _____

3) _____

Thesis:

FIRST BODY PARAGRAPH

Main idea:

Supporting evidence:

1) _____

2) _____

3) _____

SECOND BODY PARAGRAPH

Main idea:

Supporting evidence:

1) _____

2) _____

3) _____

THIRD BODY PARAGRAPH

Main idea:

Supporting evidence:

1) _____

2) _____

3) _____

CONCLUSION

Thesis restated:

Why are the ideas in this paper important?

1) _____

2) _____

3) _____

STRATEGY 31. Conferring

WRITING FOCUS: Students will get specific help on areas of need in their writing and formulate next steps for revision.

COMMON CORE ALIGNMENT: Develop and strengthen writing as needed by planning, revising, editing, rewriting, or trying a new approach, focusing on addressing what is most significant for a specific purpose and audience. (WHST.9-10.5)

RATIONALE

Meeting one-on-one with students is often the most effective way to help a student improve his or her writing. Feedback is most helpful for students when it is both oral and written, and conferences allow for both. Conferences can be short, especially if everyone comes prepared, and they typically happen during class time. They can be in the form of a conversation, where students are given time to explain their thinking. For students who need special assistance, you might also confer with them outside of class time.

As you confer with students to respond and give feedback, remember that your focus is broader than this specific essay. You are teaching "the writer, not the writing."[10] Name and celebrate students' growth and persistence as writers.

PROCEDURE

1. **Setting Up Effective Conditions for Conferring.** One of the most important questions to think about when deciding to confer with students about their writing is: What will the rest of the class do while I am working one-on-one with students? Often teachers give students time in class to work independently on their papers or other coursework while conferences take place. Sometimes teachers schedule individual student conferences during a class test. Teachers can also invite parents or other volunteers to help out with the rest of the class on days when conferences will take place. Conferences do not work well if the teacher is constantly interrupted by off-task students, so be sure to plan this time well.

2. **Preparing for the Conference.** Conferences also work best when students use this time wisely. They only get a few minutes (typically five minutes) with the teacher, so this time should focus on areas where the student has questions and/or needs help moving to the next level. Students should bring at least three specific concerns to the conference. Sentence starters that students can complete prior to the conference include:

   - *I am confused by . . .*
   - *I don't know how to . . .*
   - *I need help with . . .*
   - *I am stuck by . . .*
   - *How can I make _____ better?*

---

10 Lucy Calkins, *The Art of Teaching Writing* (Portsmouth, NH: Heinemann, 1994).

To help complete these statements, students should edit their own papers prior to the conference and/or have their papers edited by a peer. Students should bring these editing sheets to the conference.

3. **Conferring.** Students can begin the conference by explaining where they need help. When you have time to read papers in advance, you can also present one or two areas you would like to address during the conference. During the conference, many teachers help students complete a "next steps" card or section on their editing sheet, which details exactly what the student plans on doing after the conference. Students should leave a conference with two or three next steps. More than that is usually overwhelming.

4. **Post-Conference.** After conferences are over, you might debrief with the class about how the conferences went. What makes for successful conferences? What could students and the teacher do better next time? These reflections can happen in writing or through a class discussion. They often provide helpful ideas that can be used to improve conferences the next time around.

STRATEGY 32. Read-Alouds

WRITING FOCUS: Students will read another paper and provide specific feedback. They will also receive feedback on their own writing.

COMMON CORE ALIGNMENT: Develop and strengthen writing as needed by planning, revising, editing, rewriting, or trying a new approach, focusing on addressing what is most significant for a specific purpose and audience. (WHST.9-10.5)

RATIONALE

Hearing papers read aloud can be a helpful step in the editing process because it often allows us to notice things we may miss when reading a paper silently.

PROCEDURE

1. **Have Students Pair Up.** While students can read their own paper aloud, it can also be more useful for them to hear their paper read by someone else. It is best to pair students up for this exercise.

2. **Read-Aloud (Round One).** Have students take turns hearing their paper read aloud. Before students begin, you might want to model an appropriate speed at which to read so that the listener can process the information.

3. **Note-Taking and Debrief.** After hearing their papers read aloud, students should take a few minutes to record notes on their essay about sections they want to revise. They may even read sentences aloud to themselves a second time.

4. **Repeat.** Repeat this process to give both students the opportunity to hear their paper read aloud.

G. PUBLISHING/SHARING/REFLECTING

*Use these strategies **after** the unit.*

It is important to end the CWA process with an opportunity for students to share what they wrote with their peers or an outside audience. Thinkers write for many purposes; the purpose of formal writing is to express an idea to an audience. In this section, we include strategies and suggestions for how students can make their thinking public. We also include ways that students can think about what they learned about the topic and about themselves as writers.

STRATEGY 33. Reflecting on the Process

WRITING FOCUS: Students will reflect on the writing journey, celebrate their successes, and formulate a plan for growing in their writing.

COMMON CORE ALIGNMENT: Write routinely over extended time frames (time for reflection and revision) and shorter time frames (a single sitting or a day or two) for a range of discipline-specific tasks, purposes and audiences. (WHST.9-10.10)

RATIONALE

The purpose of formal writing is to share one's ideas with readers. When students have engaged in authentic inquiry about a topic, they need an authentic audience. Giving students time to reflect on their writing helps them learn more about their thinking and their writing styles. It also allows students to pause and celebrate the aspects of their writing they are proud of, which in turn will encourage them to approach the next writing task with confidence. Finally, it can also help them discover the gaps in their writing skills and make them more aware of their personal needs when writing another formal paper.

PROCEDURE

In journals, ask students to answer as many of the questions as they can. Have them attach their thinking to the final draft of their essays.

1. What aspect of your paper makes you the most proud?
2. What would you do differently next time? Why?
3. After working on this paper, what have you learned about being a good writer and the journey of writing?
4. What was the biggest challenge for you?
5. What tools or activities helped you write this paper?
6. What could you have done to help yourself write a better essay?
7. What else could have helped you write a better paper? What other support would you have liked from your peers or teacher?
8. What do you need to learn to take your writing to the next level?
9. Do you think being able to present your ideas clearly in writing is important? Why or why not?
10. What surprised you about writing this paper?

STRATEGY 34. Online Publishing

WRITING FOCUS: Students will share their work with a broader audience through the Internet or an internal website.

COMMON CORE ALIGNMENT: Use technology, including the Internet, to produce, publish, and update individual or shared writing products, taking advantage of technology's capacity to link to other information and to display information flexibly and dynamically. (WHST.9-10.6)

RATIONALE

Students need to share their work with an authentic audience outside of their classroom. This will help them to gather additional feedback and evaluate the power and potential of their writing.

Currently, over half of teenagers produce content for the Internet, and having students think critically about how, why, and where they share content can help students be better overall producers and consumers of online content.

PROCEDURE

1. **Share this video** of EdTech teacher Justin Reich speaking about using web 2.0 tools with students (see www.facinghistory.org/prompts-strategies/links to watch the video).[11] Have students consider the following: In this clip, Justin Reich states that the audience for your class work should not just be your teacher, but a wider global audience. Do you agree with his ideas? Why or why not?

2. **Thinking about Audience.** Teacher and students should think about what of their writing they would like to share with a larger audience and why. For example, students could choose the work they are most proud of, or the class could vote on a few pieces. Some guiding questions might include: Who did you think was the audience for your work on this writing project? Does knowing you will have a particular audience (outside of your teacher) require you to change or adapt your writing? Why or why not? Can you add additional resources (through links or images) that would enhance the online presence of your writing?

3. **Exploring Online Platforms.** Once students decide on an audience they want to share their work with, students may need to explore what sites, forums, or tools could help them reach that audience. Students could work in small groups to search sites that match their intended audiences. Have students search three to five sites with search key words the teacher and group come up with and then answer the following questions about each site.

    - Who runs this site?

    - What is the reputation of the organization or site?

---

[11] Justin Reich, co-director of EdTechTeacher (http://www.edtechteacher.org/), and author of *Best Ideas for Teaching with Technology: A Practical Guide for Teachers by Teachers,* is a doctoral candidate at the Harvard University School of Education and project manager of the Digital Collaborative Learning Communities Project, funded by the Hewlett Foundation.

- How is this site used and by whom?
- Could I/would I use this to share my schoolwork?
- Would I receive feedback from this site?
- What might be the benefits or drawbacks from sharing on this site?

4. Once students have explored their sites and compared answers to the questions, bring all students back to the larger group to share their findings, being sure to explain at least one of the sites to the rest of the class, including what they explored and how it works. Students and teacher may decide that their writing does not fit an external site they explored. This realization can be an important one because it shows students thinking critically about their work, the audience, and the responsibility and vulnerability that come from sharing online.

5. The class may decide to share within the school or between classes by setting up their own internal website. This would allow student work to be posted and commented on by classmates. This approach can give students a similar experience within a controlled environment. Below are some sites you may want to employ for class writing projects.

- **Wikispaces** is a social writing platform specifically for those in education.
- **Edublogs** and **Blogger** are two blog publishing-tools.
- **Ning** offers many possibilities for using social networks.

APPENDIX

SAMPLE ROAD MAP FOR *CIVIL RIGHTS HISTORICAL INVESTIGATIONS* AND THE COMMON CORE

Civil Rights Historical Investigations is a four- to six-week curriculum that asks students to investigate three case studies during the civil rights movement.

Overview

This curriculum unit is comprised of three case studies that require students to "do" history, i.e. to gather evidence from primary documents, use that evidence to make claims about the past, and then apply what they learn to their own lives today. In the first case study, students learn about how the conscious of a country was shaken by the story of Emmett Till and how the historical context surrounding his death contributed to the growth of the civil rights movement in the 1950s. In the second case study, students explore voter discrimination in the South and the philosophy of nonviolence that guided civil rights activists' responses to this injustice, culminating in the march from Selma to Montgomery in 1965. The third case study exposes students to the civil rights movement in the North by focusing on the struggle over school desegregation in Boston in the 1960s and early 1970s.

Each case study includes curriculum for a unit assessment as well as several suggested informal assessments. In addition, overall writing assignments are included as culminating assessments for the entire curriculum. Specifically, the entire unit requires students to use primary source documents and a deep study of history in order to write argumentative and informative essays. Materials are provided that scaffold both the reading, writing, and speaking and listening assignments so that students build literacy skills as they develop their understanding of this history and connect to their own lives. The unit provides teachers with the tools that they will need to engage students in learning of both the historical content and literacy skills.

Common Core Focus Standards covered

(For a complete list of all standards covered, see attached matrices.)

- RH.9-10.2 Determine the central ideas or information of a primary or secondary source; provide an accurate summary of how key events or ideas develop over the course of the text.
- RH.9-10.3 Analyze in detail a series of events described in a text; determine whether earlier events caused later ones or simply preceded them.

- RH.9-10.4 Determine the meaning of words and phrases as they are used in a text, including vocabulary describing political, social, or economic aspects of history/social science.
- RH.9-10.6 Compare the point of view of two or more authors for how they treat the same or similar topics, including which details they include and emphasize in their respective accounts.
- RH.9-10.9 Compare and contrast treatments of the same topic in several primary and secondary sources.
- WHST.9-10.1 Write arguments focused on *discipline-specific content.*
- WHST.9-10.2 Write informative/explanatory texts, including the narration of historical events, scientific procedures/ experiments, or technical processes.
- WHST.9-10.4 Produce clear and coherent writing in which the development, organization, and style are appropriate to task, purpose, and audience.
- WHST.9-10.9 Draw evidence from informational texts to support analysis, reflection, and research.
- SL.9-10.1 Initiate and participate effectively in a range of collaborative discussions (one-on-one, in groups, and teacher-led) with diverse partners on grades 9–10 topics, texts, and issues, building on others' ideas and expressing their own clearly and persuasively.

Suggested Student Objectives

- Understand the historical core concepts *significance, causation, agency, evidence,* and *continuity and change* to deepen historical understanding and explain how and why choices or events occurred during the civil rights movement
- Analyze how individuals' actions are influenced by their historical context and vice versa
- Identify choices made by people involved in this moment in history and the consequence of those choices
- Understand the philosophy of nonviolence that was a hallmark of the civil rights movement in the South
- Explore the American postwar historical context
- Analyze the use of court mandates as a remedy for school segregation
- Gather relevant information from primary source documents
- Use historical evidence to defend an argument in writing
- Write a formal paper to argue or to inform

A Sampling of Included "Texts"

(including primary sources, videos, and secondary sources)

- *Eyes on the Prize: America's Civil Rights Movement: 1954–1985*
- Library of Congress, "The Civil Rights Era in the *US News & World Report* Photographs Collection"
- "Mamie Till-Mobley Goes Public," from *Eyes on the Prize* study guide, pp. 16–17
- Excerpt from "Lynch Law in Georgia" by Ida B. Wells, 1899
- "1964: Three Civil Rights Activists Found Dead," BBC News (link in guide)
- "I Didn't Know Anything about Voting," Fannie Lou Hamer on the Mississippi Voter Registration Campaign
- "Nonviolence and Racial Justice" by Martin Luther King, Jr.
- 15th Amendment to the Constitution
- "Desegregation: Responses to the Court Order," from EOTP Study Guide, pp. 196–198
- *Milliken v. Bradley* decision

Sample Activities and Assessments

Reporter's notebook

Write an informative newspaper article about the conditions of Boston Public Schools in the 1960s. Using *Eyes on the Prize* and other primary and secondary sources, research the conditions in Boston Public Schools in the 1960s. Explain why in the 1960s, most of Boston's public schools are racially segregated. Identify steps taken by a diverse group of community members to create more racially balanced schools and the responses to these actions by the Boston School Committee. (WHST.9-10.2, RH.9-10.1, RH.9-10.9)

Emmett Till essay

Consider why the murder of Emmett Till had such a significant impact on many Americans. What decisions made by particular individuals helped make this a pivotal historical moment? What decisions most contributed to the lasting impact of this event? Write an argumentative essay using three to six pieces of textual evidence to support an original thesis. (WHST.9-10.1, RH.9-10.2, RH.9-10.6)

Timeline activity

In groups, analyze photographs, quotes, and texts from the 1960s. After watching a clip from *Eyes on the Prize*, construct a timeline of Boston's school desegregation history, giving particular attention to cause-and-effect relationships between events. (RH.9-10.3, SL.9-10.1)

Digital research of primary and secondary sources

In groups, investigate a collection of primary and secondary sources online to answer these questions: How did the historical context—the United States in the 1950s—contribute to the impact of the murder of Emmett Till? What aspects of the historical context most contributed to the lasting impact of the event? (SL.9-10.1, RH.9-10.2, RH.9-10.6)

Read and analyze a primary source

Read the essay by Martin Luther King, Jr., "Nonviolence and Racial Justice," to create a working definition for nonviolence. Investigate the text several times to understand meaning, purpose, and connection to the struggle for voting rights. (RH.9-10.4, RH.9-10.5)

Common Writing Assignment

Some people believe individuals have the power to change society. Others believe individuals are powerless to change society. Which statement does the history of the civil rights movement best support? Write an argumentative essay using three to six pieces of textual evidence to support an original thesis. (WHST.9-10.1, WHST.9-10.5)

Key Terms

- nonviolence
- agency
- causation
- pivotal
- individual and Society
- we and they
- choosing to participate
- levers of power
- powerful/powerless
- bystander
- resistance
- upstander

COMMON CORE STANDARDS CORRELATION

Civil Rights Historical Investigations • **Alignment with Common Core State Standards**

English Language Arts Standards, Writing in History/Social Studies, Grades 9–10

Text Types and Purposes

- W.9-10.1. Write arguments to support claims in an analysis of substantive topics or texts, using valid reasoning and relevant and sufficient evidence.
  - » Introduce precise claim(s), distinguish the claim(s) from alternate or opposing claims, and create an organization that establishes clear relationships among claim(s), counterclaims, reasons, and evidence.
  - » Develop claim(s) and counterclaims fairly, supplying evidence for each while pointing out the strengths and limitations of both in a manner that anticipates the audience's knowledge level and concerns.
  - » Use words, phrases, and clauses to link the major sections of the text, create cohesion, and clarify the relationships between claim(s) and reasons, between reasons and evidence, and between claim(s) and counterclaims.
  - » Establish and maintain a formal style and objective tone while attending to the norms and conventions of the discipline in which they are writing.
  - » Provide a concluding statement or section that follows from and supports the argument presented.

- W.9-10.2. Write informative/explanatory texts to examine and convey complex ideas, concepts, and information clearly and accurately through the effective selection, organization, and analysis of content.
  - » Introduce a topic; organize complex ideas, concepts, and information to make important connections and distinctions; include formatting (e.g., headings), graphics (e.g., figures, tables), and multimedia when useful to aiding comprehension.
  - » Develop the topic with well-chosen, relevant, and sufficient facts, extended definitions, concrete details, quotations, or other information and examples appropriate to the audience's knowledge of the topic.
  - » Use appropriate and varied transitions to link the major sections of the text, create cohesion, and clarify the relationships among complex ideas and concepts.
  - » Use precise language and domain-specific vocabulary to manage the complexity of the topic.
  - » Establish and maintain a formal style and objective tone while attending to the norms and conventions of the discipline in which they are writing.

» Provide a concluding statement or section that follows from and supports the information or explanation presented (e.g., articulating implications or the significance of the topic).

- W.9-10.3. Write narratives to develop real or imagined experiences or events using effective technique, well-chosen details, and well-structured event sequences.

  » Engage and orient the reader by setting out a problem, situation, or observation, establishing one or multiple point(s) of view, and introducing a narrator and/or characters; create a smooth progression of experiences or events.

  » Use narrative techniques, such as dialogue, pacing, description, reflection, and multiple plot lines, to develop experiences, events, and/or characters.

  » Use a variety of techniques to sequence events so that they build on one another to create a coherent whole.

  » Use precise words and phrases, telling details, and sensory language to convey a vivid picture of the experiences, events, setting, and/or characters.

  » Provide a conclusion that follows from and reflects on what is experienced, observed, or resolved over the course of the narrative.

Production and Distribution of Writing

- W.9-10.4. Produce clear and coherent writing in which the development, organization, and style are appropriate to task, purpose, and audience. (Grade-specific expectations for writing types are defined in the first three standards above.)

- W.9-10.5. Develop and strengthen writing as needed by planning, revising, editing, rewriting, or trying a new approach, focusing on addressing what is most significant for a specific purpose and audience.

- W.9-10.6. Use technology, including the Internet, to produce, publish, and update individual or shared writing products, taking advantage of technology's capacity to link to other information and to display information flexibly and dynamically.

Research to Build and Present Knowledge

- W.9-10.7. Conduct short as well as more sustained research projects to answer a question (including a self-generated question) or solve a problem; narrow or broaden the inquiry when appropriate; synthesize multiple sources on the subject, demonstrating understanding of the subject under investigation.

- W.9-10.8. Gather relevant information from multiple authoritative print and digital sources, using advanced searches effectively; assess the usefulness of each source in answering the research question; integrate information into the text selectively to maintain the flow of ideas, avoiding plagiarism and following a standard format for citation.

- W.9-10.9. Draw evidence from literary or informational texts to support analysis, reflection, and research.

» Apply *grades 9–10 Reading standards* to literature (e.g., "Analyze how an author draws on and transforms source material in a specific work [e.g., how Shakespeare treats a theme or topic from Ovid or the Bible or how a later author draws on a play by Shakespeare]").

» Apply *grades 9–10 Reading standards* to literary nonfiction (e.g., "Delineate and evaluate the argument and specific claims in a text, assessing whether the reasoning is valid and the evidence is relevant and sufficient; identify false statements and fallacious reasoning").

Range of Writing

- W.9-10.10. Write routinely over extended time frames (time for research, reflection, and revision) and shorter time frames (a single sitting or a day or two) for a range of tasks, purposes, and audiences.

English Language Arts Standards, Writing in History/Social Studies, Grades 9–10

CRHI section	WHST. 9–10.1	WHST. 9–10.2	WHST. 9–10.3	WHST. 9–10.4	WHST. 9–10.5	WHST. 9–10.6	WHST. 9–10.7	WHST. 9–10.8	WHST. 9–10.9	WHST. 9–10.10
Overview	•	•					•			•
Unit 1	•	•		•			•	•	•	•
Unit 2		•		•			•	•	•	•
Unit 3	•	•		•			•	•	•	•
CWA Supplement	•			•	•	•	•	•	•	•

Civil Rights Historical Investigations • **Alignment with Common Core State Standards**

English Language Arts Standards, Reading in History/Social Studies, Grades 9–10

Key Ideas and Details

- RH.9-10.1. Cite specific textual evidence to support analysis of primary and secondary sources, attending to such features as the date and origin of the information.

- RH.9-10.2. Determine the central ideas or information of a primary or secondary source; provide an accurate summary of how key events or ideas develop over the course of the text.

- RH.9-10.3. Analyze in detail a series of events described in a text; determine whether earlier events caused later ones or simply preceded them.

Craft and Structure

- RH.9-10.4. Determine the meaning of words and phrases as they are used in a text, including vocabulary describing political, social, or economic aspects of history/social science.

- RH.9-10.5. Analyze how a text uses structure to emphasize key points or advance an explanation or analysis.

- RH.9-10.6. Compare the point of view of two or more authors for how they treat the same or similar topics, including which details they include and emphasize in their respective accounts.

Integration of Knowledge and Ideas

- RH.9-10.7. Integrate quantitative or technical analysis (e.g., charts, research data) with qualitative analysis in print or digital text.

- RH.9-10.8. Assess the extent to which the reasoning and evidence in a text support the author's claims.

- RH.9-10.9. Compare and contrast treatments of the same topic in several primary and secondary sources.

Range of Reading and Level of Text Complexity

- RH.9-10.10. By the end of grade 10, read and comprehend history/social studies texts in the grades 9–10 text complexity band independently and proficiently.

English Language Arts Standards, Reading in History/Social Studies, Grades 9–10

CRHI section	RH. 9–10.1	RH. 9–10.2	RH. 9–10.3	RH. 9–10.4	RH. 9–10.5	RH. 9–10.6	RH. 9–10.7	RH. 9–10.8	RH. 9–10.9	RH. 9–10.10
Overview										
Unit 1	•	•	•	•		•			•	•
Unit 2	•	•	•	•					•	•
Unit 3	•	•	•	•		•			•	•
CWA Supplement	•	•	•	•		•	•			•

> *Civil Rights Historical Investigations* • **Alignment with Common Core State Standards**

English Language Arts Standards, Speaking and Listening, Grades 9–10

Comprehension and Collaboration

- SL.9-10.1. Initiate and participate effectively in a range of collaborative discussions (one-on-one, in groups, and teacher-led) with diverse partners on grades 9–10 topics, texts, and issues, building on others' ideas and expressing their own clearly and persuasively.

  » Come to discussions prepared, having read and researched material under study; explicitly draw on that preparation by referring to evidence from texts and other research on the topic or issue to stimulate a thoughtful, well-reasoned exchange of ideas.

  » Work with peers to set rules for collegial discussions and decision-making (e.g., informal consensus, taking votes on key issues, presentation of alternate views), clear goals and deadlines, and individual roles as needed.

  » Propel conversations by posing and responding to questions that relate the current discussion to broader themes or larger ideas; actively incorporate others into the discussion; and clarify, verify, or challenge ideas and conclusions.

  » Respond thoughtfully to diverse perspectives, summarize points of agreement and disagreement, and, when warranted, qualify or justify their own views and understanding and make new connections in light of the evidence and reasoning presented.

- SL.9-10.2. Integrate multiple sources of information presented in diverse media or formats (e.g., visually, quantitatively, orally) evaluating the credibility and accuracy of each source.

- SL.9-10.3. Evaluate a speaker's point of view, reasoning, and use of evidence and rhetoric, identifying any fallacious reasoning or exaggerated or distorted evidence.

Presentation of Knowledge and Ideas

- SL.9-10.4. Present information, findings, and supporting evidence clearly, concisely, and logically such that listeners can follow the line of reasoning and the organization, development, substance, and style are appropriate to purpose, audience, and task.

- SL.9-10.5. Make strategic use of digital media (e.g., textual, graphical, audio, visual, and interactive elements) in presentations to enhance understanding of findings, reasoning, and evidence and to add interest.

- SL.9-10.6. Adapt speech to a variety of contexts and tasks, demonstrating command of formal English when indicated or appropriate.

English Language Arts Standards, Speaking and Listening, Grades 9–10

CRHI section	SL.9–10.1	SL. 9–10.2	SL. 9–10.3	SL. 9–10.4	SL. 9–10.5	SL. 9–10.6
Overview				•		•
Unit 1	•					•
Unit 2	•	•		•		•
Unit 3	•	•				•
CWA Supplement	•	•	•	•		•

Sample High School Rubric for Argumentative Writing Prompts

	4 (Advanced)	3 (Proficient)	2 (Needs Improvement)	1 (Warning)
Introduction and Thesis Statement Total: _____	☐ Introduction provides excellent historical context and preview for the essay. ☐ Clear, supportable thesis (claim) that responds to the prompt.	☐ Introduction provides adequate context and preview for the essay. ☐ Clear, supportable thesis (claim) that responds to the prompt.	☐ Introduction attempts to provide context and preview for the essay. ☐ Thesis (claim) lacks clarity and/or is partially supportable. ☐ Thesis (claim) may not respond fully to the prompt.	☐ Introduction provides little context or preview for the essay. ☐ Thesis (claim) unclear and/or is not supportable. ☐ Thesis (claim) does not respond to the prompt.
Evidence and Support Total: _____	☐ Strong, supportive examples demonstrate deep understanding of the historical issue. ☐ Evidence strongly supports the thesis (claim).	☐ Appropriate, supportive examples which demonstrate understanding of the historical issue. ☐ Evidence supports the thesis (claim).	☐ Supportive examples attempted but demonstrate a lack of understanding of the historical issue. ☐ Evidence does not fully support the thesis (claim).	☐ Evidence nonexistent, irrelevant, and/or inaccurate. ☐ No sources or sources are of poor quality.
Argument and Analysis Total: _____	☐ Thoroughly develops argument. ☐ Addresses counterarguments fairly (while pointing out the strengths and limitations of both argument(s) and counterarguments.) ☐ Consistently provides clear analysis of how the evidence supports the thesis. ☐ Thorough discussion of relevant historical context. ☐ The reader can easily follow the writer's logical progression from one point to the next.	☐ Adequately develops argument. ☐ Addresses counterarguments (may point out the strengths and limitations of both argument(s) and counterarguments.) ☐ Provides clear analysis of how the evidence supports the thesis. ☐ Adequate discussion of relevant historical context. ☐ The reader can follow the writer's logical progression from one point to the next.	☐ Attempts to develop argument. ☐ Limited attempt to address counterarguments (may not point out the strengths and limitations of both argument(s) and counterarguments.) ☐ Provides some analysis of how the evidence supports the thesis. ☐ Inadequate discussion of relevant historical context. ☐ It is difficult to identify a logical pattern throughout the essay.	☐ Argument is very limited and/or not developed. ☐ Little to no attempt to address counterarguments (does not point out the strengths and limitations of both argument(s) and counterarguments.) ☐ Provides little to no analysis of how the evidence supports the argument ☐ Little to no discussion of relevant historical context. ☐ Logical pattern may not be present.
Writing/ Organization/ Conventions Total: _____	☐ Strong use of language to create cohesion and clarify the relationships among claims, counterclaims, reasons, and evidence. ☐ All paragraphs develop a single point introduced by a topic sentence. ☐ Excellent sequencing and transitions. ☐ Strong conclusion which supports the thesis (claim). ☐ Virtually free of errors in mechanics, usage, grammar, and spelling. ☐ High quality sources cited appropriately (MLA or APA) ☐ Typed.	☐ Adequate use of language to create cohesion and clarify the relationships among claims, counterclaims, reasons, and evidence. ☐ Most paragraphs develop a single point introduced by a topic sentence. ☐ Adequate sequencing and transitions. ☐ Adequate conclusion which supports the thesis (claim). ☐ Minor errors in mechanics, usage, grammar, and spelling. ☐ Quality sources cited appropriately (MLA or APA). ☐ Typed.	☐ Inadequate use of language to create cohesion and clarify the relationships among claims, counterclaims, reasons, and evidence. ☐ Some paragraphs develop a single point introduced by a topic sentence. ☐ Inadequate sequencing and transitions. ☐ Attempts a conclusion which is related to the thesis (claim). ☐ Frequent errors in mechanics, usage, grammar, and spelling. ☐ Limited sources and/or attempts a standard citation format (MLA or APA) ☐ Handwritten.	☐ Lacking language which creates cohesion in relationships among claims, counterclaims, reasons, and evidence. ☐ Few paragraphs develop a single point introduced by a topic sentence. ☐ Lacks sequencing and transitions. ☐ Limited conclusion and/or may not relate to thesis. ☐ Severe errors in mechanics, usage, grammar, and spelling. ☐ No sources and/or no standard citation format. ☐ Handwritten.

TEACHER COMMENTS:
☐ Check here if the student did not complete the Common Writing Assignment or if their work was plagiarized.

TOTAL: _____ / _____